EASY MEDITERR

DIET FOR BEGINNERS

Tasty Recipes for a Balanced Lifestyle

Samuel Hayes

TABLE OF CONTENTS

WELCOME TO THE MEDITERRANEAN DIET!

Congratulations on embarking on your journey towards a healthier and tastier way of living. The Mediterranean slim down isn't around what you eat; it's too approximately increasing in value and getting a charge out of the Mediterranean region's delicious nourishment and cooking styles.

With its emphasis on fresh and wholesome ingredients, this diet is delicious and known for its numerous health benefits.

The eating habits of people in countries like Greece, Italy, Spain, and Morocco inspire the Mediterranean diet. A wide array of vegetables, whole grains, fruits, nuts, seeds, and olive oil characterizes it. Fish and poultry are preferred over meat, and dairy products are often moderately enjoyed. This diet is not about strict restrictions; instead, it encourages a balanced and enjoyable approach to food.

In this cookbook, we have carefully curated 70 easy-to-follow recipes perfect for beginners looking to explore the wonders of the Mediterranean diet. Regardless of your culinary expertise, these recipes will ignite your passion for cooking, guiding you to craft delightful dishes that nurture your body and spirit.

You will discover the joy of savoring vibrant flavors, the satisfaction of preparing meals with love, and the pleasure of sharing these culinary experiences with loved ones. It's not just a diet but a lifestyle promoting overall well-being and a strong sense of community.

Each chapter in this cookbook is designed to guide you through various meal occasions, from hearty breakfasts to refreshing juices and smoothies and from satisfying main dishes to delectable desserts. Along the way, you'll learn about the health benefits of key ingredients and how to incorporate them into your daily meals.

So, whether you're cooking for yourself, your partner, or your family, we hope these recipes become a source of inspiration, joy, and good health. Let the Mediterranean diet be your gateway to a healthier, happier, and more delicious life.

Thank you for joining us on this culinary adventure. Let's savor the flavors of the Mediterranean together!

BENEFITS OF THE MEDITERRANEAN DIET

The Mediterranean Diet offers a plethora of benefits that extend beyond just the delight of enjoying delectable dishes. This eating pattern has been celebrated and studied for its positive impact on overall health and well-being. Here are some of the remarkable benefits you can experience by adopting the Mediterranean Diet:

1. Eating foods like olive oil, nuts, and fish that have healthy fats can make your heart healthier. Research has indicated that if you eat a Mediterranean Diet, you have a lower chance of getting heart problems, and your bad cholesterol levels decrease.

2. Weight Management: The abundance of fresh fruits, vegetables, and whole grains in the Mediterranean Diet, coupled with the moderate consumption of lean proteins and healthy fats, can support weight management efforts. Additionally, the diet's focus on mindful eating and enjoyment of meals can promote better portion control.

3. Diabetes Prevention: The Mediterranean Diet's nutrient-dense and fiber-rich foods can help regulate blood sugar levels, making it beneficial for individuals at risk of type 2 diabetes. This eating plan may improve insulin sensitivity and reduce the risk of developing diabetes.

4. Brain Health: The diet's inclusion of antioxidants, vitamins, and minerals from various colorful fruits and vegetables contributes to better cognitive function and a reduced risk of age-related cognitive decline.

5. Reduced Inflammation: The anti-inflammatory properties of many Mediterranean Diet ingredients, such as olive oil and fatty fish, may help alleviate chronic inflammation.

6. Digestive Health: Eating foods like whole grains, fruits, and vegetables in the Mediterranean Diet can be good for our digestion. These foods contain a good amount of fiber that can help avoid constipation and maintain a healthy gut.

7. Longevity: Research suggests that adhering to the Mediterranean Diet is associated with increased life expectancy and a reduced risk of premature death.

8. Nutrient-Rich: This diet is abundant in vitamins, minerals, and essential nutrients that nourish the body, providing a well-rounded and balanced approach to eating.
9. Improved Skin Health: Eating healthy fats and antioxidants in the Mediterranean Diet can help make your skin look healthy and glowing. It does this by protecting it from damage and helping it produce collagen.
10. Emotional Well-Being: The social aspect of enjoying meals with family and friends, a hallmark of the Mediterranean lifestyle, contributes to a sense of community and enhanced emotional well-being.

By embracing the Mediterranean Diet, you'll not only savor the delicious flavors of the Mediterranean region but also nourish your body and enhance your quality of life. So, dive into the Mediterranean way of eating and enjoy it!

ESSENTIAL INGREDIENTS AND COOKING TECHNIQUES

Mastering the Mediterranean Diet starts with understanding its essential ingredients and cooking techniques. This wholesome culinary approach emphasizes fresh, nutrient-dense foods and simple yet flavorful preparation methods. Here are the key elements and cooking practices to bring the essence of the Mediterranean to your kitchen:

Essential Ingredients:

1. Olive Oil: Considered the heart of the Mediterranean Diet, use extra-virgin olive oil as your primary cooking fat and drizzle it over salads and dishes for its rich flavor and health benefits.

2. Fresh Fruits and Vegetables: Embrace a colorful array of seasonal fruits and vegetables as they form the foundation of your meals, providing essential vitamins, minerals, and antioxidants.

3. Whole Grains: Elect entirety grains like quinoa, bulgur, farro, and brown rice, which are wealthy in fiber and supplements. They include a healthy component to your dishes and advance stomach-related well-being.

4. Legumes and Beans: Packed with protein, fiber, and vital nutrients, beans, lentils, and chickpeas are versatile ingredients, ideal for soups, stews, salads, and more.

5. Fish and Fish: Greasy angles such as salmon, mackerel, and sardines give omega-3 greasy acids and contribute to heart well-being. Join them in your eating less frequently.

6. Poultry and Lean Meats: While red meat is consumed in moderation, prioritize lean cuts of poultry and limit the intake of processed meats.

7. Nuts and Seeds: Include a modest bunch of nuts and seeds in your everyday snacking schedule, advertising solid fats and different benefits.

8. Herbs and Spices: Elevate your dishes with Mediterranean herbs like basil, oregano, rosemary, and thyme, along with cumin, coriander, and paprika.

9. Dairy and Dairy Alternatives: Choose yogurt and cheese in moderation, and consider plant-based dairy alternatives like almond milk or soy milk.

Cooking Techniques:

1. Grilling: Grill fish, vegetables, and poultry for a smoky flavor and minimal use of oil.
2. Roasting: Roast vegetables and fruits to enhance their natural sweetness and create depth in flavors.
3. Sauteing: Saute onions, garlic, and vegetables with olive oil for a base of many Mediterranean dishes.
4. Steaming: Steam vegetables retain their nutrients and vibrant colors.
5. Simmering: Use slow, gentle simmering to develop rich flavors in soups, stews, and sauces.
6. Marinating: Marinate meats and fish with herbs, spices, and citrus for added taste and tenderness.
7. Dressing: Create homemade sauces with olive oil, lemon juice, and herbs to elevate salads.
8. Baking: Bake whole grains, fish, and vegetables for a delicious, healthier alternative to frying.
9. Blending: Blend fruits and vegetables into smoothies and purees for refreshing beverages and sauces.

By incorporating these essential ingredients and cooking techniques into your culinary repertoire, you'll be well on your way to mastering the Mediterranean Diet and enjoying a delectable, healthful, and vibrant way of eating.

TIPS AND TRICKS FOR MAKING MEDITERRANEAN EATING A PART OF YOUR DAILY ROUTINE:

Congratulations on embarking on the Mediterranean Diet journey! Now, let's delve into some practical tips and tricks to seamlessly incorporate this wholesome and delicious way of eating into your daily routine:

1. Start Gradually: Transitioning to a new dietary pattern takes time. Gradually increase by incorporating one or two Mediterranean-inspired meals into your weekly menu.

2. Shop Smart: Stock your pantry and refrigerator with Mediterranean staples like olive oil, whole grains, beans, nuts, and fresh fruits and vegetables. Having these items readily available will make meal planning easier.

3. Embrace Seasonal Produce: Celebrate the changing seasons by incorporating locally grown, seasonal fruits and vegetables into your meals. Not only will this support local farmers, but it will also add variety and freshness to your dishes.

4. Create Balanced Meals: Aim to include a diverse array of colors, flavors, and textures in your meals. Balance your plate with vegetables, grains, lean proteins, and healthy fats to create satisfying and nutritious meals.

5. Savor the Flavors: The Mediterranean Diet is all about enjoying the natural flavors of wholesome ingredients. Experiment with herbs, spices, and citrus to enhance the taste of your dishes without relying on excessive salt or unhealthy additives.

6. Cook with Family and Friends: Engage loved ones in the cooking process. Preparing meals together can be a fun and bonding experience while fostering a sense of community around food.

7. Plan: Set aside weekly time to plan your meals and snacks. A meal plan can help you stick to healthy eating goals and avoid sudden, unhealthy food choices.

8. Make sure you drink lots of water throughout the day to stay hydrated. For a refreshing twist, infuse your water with slices of citrus fruits, cucumbers, or herbs.

9. Enjoy Regular Physical Activity: Alongside a balanced diet, regular exercise is vital for overall well-being. Incorporate enjoyable activities like walking, swimming, or yoga to maintain a healthy lifestyle.

10. Practice Mindful Eating: Slow down during meals, savor each bite, and be present in the moment. Mindful eating promotes better digestion and helps you recognize when you're full, preventing overeating.

11. Be Kind to Yourself: Remember that dietary changes take time, and it's okay to have occasional indulgences. Don't feel discouraged by setbacks; celebrate your progress and focus on positive changes.

By incorporating these tips and tricks into your daily routine, you'll find that embracing the Mediterranean Diet becomes a natural and enjoyable part of your lifestyle. Embrace the journey, savor the flavors, and nourish your body with the bountiful benefits of this time-honored and healthful way of eating.

CHAPTER 1: BREAKFAST RECIPES

CLASSIC GREEK YOGURT PARFAIT

Prep Time: 10 minutes. Servings: 2

Ingredients:

- 1 cup Greek yogurt
- 1/2 cup granola
- One cup of various fresh berries like strawberries, blueberries, and raspberries.
- 2 tablespoons honey
- 1/4 teaspoon vanilla extract
- 2 tablespoons finely chopped nuts (almonds or walnuts, for example)

Directions:

1. Combine the Greek yogurt with honey and vanilla extract in a small bowl, ensuring they are thoroughly mixed. Set the mixture aside for later use.
2. Layer the Greek yogurt mixture, granola, and mixed fresh berries in two serving glasses or bowls. Keep adding the ingredients in layers until the glass is filled.
3. Top each parfait with chopped nuts for added crunch and flavor.
4. Serve immediately or refrigerate for a few hours to allow the flavors to meld together.

Nutrition Info (per serving):

- Calories: 300
- Protein: 12g
- Fat: 8g
- Carbohydrates: 48g
- Fiber: 5g
- Sugar: 22g
- Sodium: 80mg

MEDITERRANEAN OMELETTE WITH SPINACH AND FETA

Prep Time: 10 minutes Cook Time: 10 minutes Servings: 2

Ingredients:

- 4 large eggs
- 1/4 cup crumbled feta cheese
- 1 cup fresh spinach leaves, chopped
- 1/4 cup cherry tomatoes, halved
- 1/4 cup chopped red bell pepper
- 2 tablespoons chopped red onion
- 1 tablespoon chopped fresh parsley
- 1 tablespoon olive oil
- Salt and pepper to taste

Directions:

1. In a bowl, whisk the eggs until well beaten—season with a pinch of salt and pepper.
2. Warm the olive oil in a pan that doesn't stick on medium heat until it's warm. Sauté the chopped red onion and bell pepper for 2-3 minutes until they turn soft and tender.
3. Put the cut spinach and cherry tomatoes into the pan. Continue cooking for 2 minutes more until the spinach starts to shrink a little.
4. Put the mixed eggs on top of the vegetables in the frying pan. Tilt the pan to ensure the eggs spread evenly.
5. Cook the omelet for about 4-5 minutes until the edges are set, and the center is slightly runny.
6. Evenly scatter the crumbled feta cheese over half of the omelet.
7. Gently fold the other half of the omelet over the side containing the feta cheese, forming a half-moon shape.
8. Cook for another 1-2 minutes until the cheese melts and the omelet is fully cooked.
9. Slide the Mediterranean omelet onto a plate and garnish with chopped fresh parsley.
10. Serve hot as a delicious and nutritious Mediterranean-inspired breakfast or brunch option.

Nutrition Info (per serving):

- Calories: 220
- Protein: 14g
- Fat: 15g
- Carbohydrates: 6g
- Fiber: 2g
- Sugar: 3g
- Sodium: 320mg

TOMATO AND BASIL FRITTATA

Prep Time: 10 minutes Cook Time: 20 minutes Servings: 4

Ingredients:

- 6 large eggs
- 1 cup cherry tomatoes, halved
- 1/4 cup fresh basil leaves, chopped
- 1/4 cup grated Parmesan cheese
- 1/4 cup diced red onion
- 2 cloves garlic, minced
- 2 tablespoons olive oil
- Salt and pepper to taste

Directions:

1. Before starting, ensure your oven is preheated to 375°F (190°C).
2. In a big bowl, mix the eggs until they are well beaten. Add a little salt and pepper.

3. Heat the olive oil in a frying pan on medium heat. The skillet should be oven-safe. Put the chopped red onion and crushed garlic together. Sauté for 2-3 minutes until the onions become translucent.
4. Put the cut cherry tomatoes in the pan and cook for 2 minutes until they become softer.
5. Put the eggs mixed over the vegetables in the pan. Sprinkle the chopped fresh basil and grated Parmesan cheese evenly over the top.
6. Let the frittata cook on the stovetop for about 5 minutes until the edges start to set.
7. Move the frying pan to the hot oven and cook for 10-12 minutes or until the frittata is completely cooked and a little bit golden.
8. Please remove the frittata from the oven and wait for it to cool a little before cutting it.
9. Serve warm as a delightful Mediterranean-inspired brunch or lunch option. You can also enjoy it cold as a delicious leftover.

Nutrition Info (per serving):

- Calories: 180
- Protein: 11g
- Fat: 12g
- Carbohydrates: 6g
- Fiber: 1g
- Sugar: 2g
- Sodium: 240mg

SPANISH PAN CON TOMATE

Prep Time: 10 minutes Cook Time: 5 minutes Servings: 4

Ingredients:

- 4 slices of rustic bread, preferably baguette or ciabatta
- 2 ripe tomatoes, halved
- 2 garlic cloves, peeled
- Extra-virgin olive oil
- Sea salt
- Freshly ground black pepper

Directions:

1. Toast the slices of rustic bread until they are lightly golden and crispy.
2. Take one-half of the ripe tomato and rub it over one side of each toasted bread slice. The juicy tomato flesh will spread and infuse the bread with flavor.
3. Rub the peeled garlic cloves gently over the tomato-rubbed side of the bread. This will add a subtle garlic aroma to the dish.
4. Drizzle a generous amount of extra-virgin olive oil over the top of each bread slice.
5. Put a little bit of sea salt and pepper on the olive oil.

6. Serve the Pan con Tomate as a delicious and authentic Spanish appetizer or accompaniment to a Mediterranean meal.

Nutrition Info (per serving):

- Calories: 150
- Protein: 3g
- Fat: 7g
- Carbohydrates: 19g
- Fiber: 2g
- Sugar: 2g
- Sodium: 220mg

MEDITERRANEAN AVOCADO TOAST

Prep Time: 10 minutes Cook Time: 5 minutes Servings: 2

Ingredients:

- 2 slices of whole-grain bread
- 1 ripe avocado, peeled and pitted
- 1 small tomato, diced
- 2 tablespoons crumbled feta cheese
- 1 tablespoon chopped fresh basil
- 1 tablespoon extra-virgin olive oil
- Juice of half a lemon
- Salt and pepper to taste

Directions:

1. Toast the slices of whole-grain bread until they are golden and crispy.
2. Take a fork and squash the soft avocado until it becomes smooth and creamy in a small bowl.

3. Spread the mashed avocado evenly over the toasted bread slices.
4. Top each avocado toast with the diced tomato, crumbled feta cheese, and chopped fresh basil.
5. Drizzle extra-virgin olive oil and lemon juice over each avocado toast.
6. Season with salt and pepper to taste.
7. Serve the Mediterranean Avocado Toast as a delicious, nutritious breakfast, snack, or light lunch.

Nutrition Info (per serving):

- Calories: 260
- Protein: 6g
- Fat: 18g
- Carbohydrates: 19g
- Fiber: 7g
- Sugar: 2g
- Sodium: 210mg

FRUIT AND NUT BREAKFAST COUSCOUS

Prep Time: 10 minutes Cook Time: 10 minutes Servings: 2

Ingredients:

- 1 cup whole wheat couscous
- 1 1/4 cups water
- 1/4 teaspoon salt
- 1/2 teaspoon ground cinnamon
- 1/4 teaspoon ground nutmeg
- 1/4 cup chopped dried apricots
- 1/4 cup chopped dried figs
- Use 1/4 of a cup of nuts cut into small pieces. You can choose from almonds, walnuts, or pistachios.1 tablespoon honey or maple syrup
- 1/2 cup plain Greek yogurt
- Fresh fruits for garnish (such as berries, sliced banana, or apple)

Directions:

1. Heat the water in a pot until it starts to bubble. Mix the couscous and salt, then put a lid on the bank and remove the heat. Wait about 5 minutes or until the couscous soaks up the water and becomes light and fluffy.
2. Cushion the cooked couscous with a fork; at that point, blend in cinnamon and ground nutmeg.
3. Add the chopped dried apricots, figs, and nuts to the couscous mixture. Mix well to distribute the fruits and nuts evenly.
4. Pour the honey or maple syrup over the couscous and mix it all.
5. To serve, divide the fruit and nut breakfast couscous into two bowls. Put a big spoonful of plain Greek yogurt on top of each bowl.
6. Garnish with fresh fruits like berries, sliced bananas, or apple slices.
7. Enjoy the delicious and nutritious Fruit and Nut Breakfast Couscous as a delightful start to your day!

Nutrition Info (per serving):

- Calories: 350
- Protein: 12g
- Fat: 8g
- Carbohydrates: 62g
- Fiber: 7g
- Sugar: 18g
- Sodium: 150mg

DATE AND WALNUT ENERGY BITES

Prep Time: 15 minutes Chilling Time: 30 minutes Servings: 12 energy bites

Ingredients:

- 1 cup pitted dates
- 1 cup walnuts
- 1/4 cup almond butter
- 1 tablespoon honey or maple syrup
- 1 teaspoon vanilla extract
- Pinch of salt
- 1/2 cup of unsweetened shredded coconut to coat the food, but it's optional.

Directions:

1. Combine the pitted dates, walnuts, almond butter, honey or maple syrup, vanilla extract, and a little salt in a food processor. Blend the mixture until it becomes sticky and even dough.
2. Take a spoonful of the dough and shape it into a small ball by rolling it with your hands. Do the same thing again with the rest of the dough to make 12 energy bites.
3. Roll the energy bites in shredded coconut to coat them for extra flavor and texture if desired.

4. Put the date and walnut energy bites on a plate or tray with parchment paper. Then, put them in the refrigerator for at least 30 minutes to become firmer.
5. After cooling down, move the energy bites to a sealed container and keep them in the fridge for seven days.
6. Enjoy these delicious Date and Walnut Energy Bites as a quick and nutritious snack on-the-go or whenever you need a natural energy boost!

Nutrition Info (per energy bite):

- Calories: 130
- Protein: 2g
- Fat: 7g
- Carbohydrates: 17g
- Fiber: 2g
- Sugar: 13g
- Sodium: 10mg

FIG AND RICOTTA BRUSCHETTA

Prep Time: 15 minutes Cook Time: 5 minutes Servings: 4

Ingredients:

- 4 slices of crusty bread (baguette or ciabatta)
- 1 cup ricotta cheese
- 8 fresh figs, sliced
- 2 tablespoons honey
- Fresh thyme leaves, for garnish
- Pinch of salt
- Pinch of black pepper

Directions:

1. Preheat the broiler in your oven.
2. Place the bread pieces on a tray and heat them under the grill for 1-2 minutes on both sides until they turn golden and crunchy.
3. Mix the ricotta cheese with a pinch of salt and black pepper in a small bowl. Stir until well combined.
4. Spread a generous layer of the seasoned ricotta cheese on each toasted bread slice.
5. Top the ricotta with sliced figs, arranging them evenly on each bruschetta.

6. Drizzle honey over the figs, allowing the sweetness to enhance the flavors.
7. Garnish with fresh thyme leaves for a hint of herbal aroma and color.
8. Serve the Fig and Ricotta Bruschetta immediately as a delicious appetizer or light snack.

Nutrition Info (per serving, one bruschetta):

- Calories: 210
- Protein: 7g
- Fat: 6g
- Carbohydrates: 35g
- Fiber: 3g
- Sugar: 18g
- Sodium: 190mg

ITALIAN BREAKFAST STRATA

Prep Time: 20 minutes Cook Time: 45 minutes Servings: 2

Ingredients:

- 4 slices of Italian bread, cubed
- 1/2 cup cherry tomatoes, halved
- 1/2 cup cooked Italian sausage, crumbled
- 1/2 cup baby spinach leaves
- 1/2 cup shredded mozzarella cheese
- 1/4 cup grated Parmesan cheese
- 3 large eggs
- 3/4 cup milk
- 1/2 teaspoon dried oregano
- 1/4 teaspoon garlic powder
- Salt and pepper to taste
- Fresh basil leaves for garnish

Directions:

1. Turn on your oven and set the temperature to 375°F (190°C). Coat a little baking dish with cooking spray or butter.
2. Place half of the cubed Italian bread at the bottom of the prepared baking dish.
3. Layer half of the cherry tomatoes, cooked Italian sausage, baby spinach, mozzarella, and Parmesan cheese on top of the bread.
4. Add the remaining bread cubes to the first layer, followed by the rest of the tomatoes, sausage, spinach, and cheese.
5. Mix the eggs, milk, dried oregano, garlic powder, salt, and pepper in a bowl.
6. Evenly pour the mixed eggs over the layered ingredients in the dish.
7. Put the foil on the dish and keep it in the refrigerator for at least 30 minutes or overnight. This allows the flavors to meld together.
8. When you're about to start baking, heat your oven to 375°F (190°C).
9. Remove the foil and bake the Italian Breakfast Strata for about 35-40 minutes, until the top is golden and the eggs are set.
10. Let the strata cool for a few minutes before slicing into portions.
11. Garnish with fresh basil leaves for added aroma and presentation.

Nutrition Info (per serving):

- Calories: 450 kcal
- Fat: 26g
- Saturated Fat: 11g
- Cholesterol: 225mg
- Sodium: 810mg
- Carbohydrates: 28g
- Fiber: 3g
- Sugar: 5g
- Protein: 27g

LEMON POPPY SEED MUFFINS

Prep Time: 10 minutes Cook Time: 18-20 minutes Servings: 12 muffins

Ingredients:

- 1 and 1/2 cups all-purpose flour
- 1/2 cup granulated sugar
- 2 teaspoons baking powder
- 1/4 teaspoon baking soda
- 1/4 teaspoon salt
- 1 tablespoon poppy seeds
- Half a cup of butter with no salt added, melted, and cooled down.
- 1/2 cup milk
- 1/4 cup fresh lemon juice
- 2 tablespoons lemon zest
- 1 large egg
- 1 teaspoon vanilla extract

Directions:

1. Please turn on your oven and set it to 350°F (175°C). Put paper liners in the muffin tin or grease the cups to stop the muffins from getting stuck.
2. Put the flour, sugar, preparing powder, preparing pop, salt, and poppy seeds in an expansive bowl and blend them.
3. Mix the melted butter, milk, lemon juice, lemon zest, egg, and vanilla extract in a different bowl until well combined.
4. Slowly include the damp fixings with the dry fixings and delicately blend until they are well combined. Avoid over-stirring the mixture. Exercise caution not to overmix the batter; it's acceptable if small lumps are present.
5. Fill the muffin cups with the batter, filling them about two-thirds full.
6. Put the muffins in the oven and leave them for 18-20 minutes or until a toothpick comes out without any batter on it.
7. Permit the biscuits to cool within the dish for 5 minutes; at that point, exchange them to a wire rack to cool totally.

Nutrition Information (per serving):

- Calories: 180 kcal
- Fat: 9g
- Saturated Fat: 5g
- Cholesterol: 35mg
- Sodium: 150mg
- Carbohydrates: 22g
- Fiber: 1g
- Sugar: 10g
- Protein: 3g

CHAPTER 2: APPETIZERS AND SNACKS

HUMMUS WITH PITA BREAD AND FRESH VEGETABLES

Prep Time: 10 minutes. Servings: 2

Ingredients:

- 1 cup cooked chickpeas (garbanzo beans), drained and rinsed
- 1/4 cup tahini
- 1/4 cup fresh lemon juice
- 2 garlic cloves, minced
- 1/2 teaspoon ground cumin
- 1/4 teaspoon paprika
- 1/4 cup extra-virgin olive oil
- Salt, to taste
- Freshly ground black pepper, to taste
- Cut 2 pita bread made with whole wheat into triangle pieces.
- Fresh vegetables (carrots, cucumber, bell peppers, etc.), sliced for dipping

Directions:

1. Combine chickpeas, tahini, lemon juice, minced garlic, ground cumin, and paprika in a nourishment processor or blender. Mix until all the ingredients are well combined and the texture is silky and smooth.
2. While the machine is on, slowly pour the extra-virgin olive oil into it until everything is mixed well. If the hummus is too thick, add water until it is the thickness you want.
3. Try the hummus and add salt and freshly ground black pepper if it needs more flavor. Change the taste according to your preference.
4. Put the hummus in a bowl and pour olive oil to make it look nice.
5. Serve the hummus with pita bread wedges and various fresh vegetable slices for dipping.

Nutrition Information (per serving):

- Calories: 360 kcal
- Total Fat: 23g
- Saturated Fat: 3g
- Trans Fat: 0g
- Cholesterol: 0mg
- Sodium: 450mg
- Total Carbohydrate: 30g
- Dietary Fiber: 6g
- Sugars: 2g
- Protein: 10g

GREEK SPANAKOPITA

Prep Time: 20 minutes. Servings: 2

Ingredients:

- 2 cups fresh spinach, chopped
- 1 cup feta cheese, crumbled
- 1/4 cup ricotta cheese
- 2 green onions, chopped
- 2 tablespoons fresh dill, chopped
- 1 tablespoon fresh parsley, chopped
- 1 tablespoon olive oil
- 1/4 teaspoon ground nutmeg
- Salt and pepper, to taste
- 4 sheets of phyllo dough
- 2 tablespoons melted butter

Directions:

1. Before cooking, turn on your oven and set the temperature to 375°F (190°C).
2. Mix the chopped spinach, crumbled feta cheese, ricotta cheese, chopped green onions, fresh dill, and parsley in a large bowl.

3. Place a small amount of olive oil onto the mixture, and then evenly distribute ground nutmeg, salt, and pepper on top. Stir all the ingredients together until they are mixed well.
4. Place a piece of phyllo dough on a clean surface and gently coat it with melted butter. Do the same thing with the rest of the Phyllo sheets. Put melted butter on each sheet before you put the next one on top.
5. Place half of the spinach and cheese filling along one edge of the phyllo stack, leaving some space around the edges. Carefully wrap the phyllo dough around the filling, fold the sides, and then roll it up like a log.
6. Repeat the same process with the second batch of phyllo and filling to make another roll.
7. Place both rolls on a baking sheet lined with parchment paper, with the seam side facing down.
8. Brush the tops of the rolls with a little more melted butter for a golden finish.
9. Bake the Spanakopita in the preheated oven for 25-30 minutes or until the phyllo is crisp and golden brown.
10. Take it out of the oven and cool before cutting each roll into two pieces.

Nutrition Information (per serving):

- Calories: 360 kcal
- Total Fat: 22g
- Saturated Fat: 12g
- Trans Fat: 0g
- Cholesterol: 65mg
- Sodium: 580mg
- Total Carbohydrate: 27g
- Dietary Fiber: 2g
- Sugars: 1g
- Protein: 16g

TOMATO AND MOZZARELLA CAPRESE SKEWERS

Prep Time: 15 minutes. Servings: 2

Ingredients:

- 1 cup cherry tomatoes
- 1 cup fresh mozzarella balls
- Fresh basil leaves
- Balsamic glaze
- Extra virgin olive oil
- Salt and pepper, to taste
- Wooden skewers

Directions:

1. Wash and dry the cherry tomatoes and basil leaves. Drain the fresh mozzarella balls if they come in liquid.
2. Thread one cherry tomato, followed by a fresh mozzarella ball, and then a basil leaf onto each wooden skewer. Repeat until all the ingredients are used.

3. Arrange the skewers on a serving platter.
4. Sprinkle balsamic coat and additional virgin olive oil over the sticks. Add salt and pepper for a better taste.
5. Serve the Tomato and Mozzarella Caprese Skewers immediately or refrigerate until ready to serve.

Nutrition Information (per serving):

- Calories: 190 kcal
- Total Fat: 13g
- Saturated Fat: 6g
- Trans Fat: 0g
- Cholesterol: 30mg
- Sodium: 320mg
- Total Carbohydrate: 7g
- Dietary Fiber: 1g
- Sugars: 4g
- Protein: 10g

MEDITERRANEAN STUFFED GRAPE LEAVES

Prep Time: 45 minutes Cook Time: 30 minutes Servings: 2

Ingredients:

- One container of grape leaves, which has approximately 30 leaves.
- 1 cup long-grain rice, rinsed and drained
- 1 small onion, finely chopped
- 2 cloves garlic, minced
- 1/4 cup fresh parsley, chopped
- 1/4 cup fresh mint, chopped
- 1/4 cup fresh dill, chopped
- 1/4 cup pine nuts (optional)
- 1/4 cup extra virgin olive oil
- Juice of 1 lemon
- Salt and pepper to taste
- Water for cooking

Directions:

1. Get the grape leaves ready: If you are using grape leaves that have been preserved, wash them with cold water to get rid of extra salt. If using fresh grape leaves, blanch them in boiling water for 1-2 minutes until they become tender. Drain and set aside.

2. In a large bowl, combine the rice, chopped onion, minced garlic, parsley, mint, dill, and pine nuts (if using).
3. Drizzle the olive oil and lemon juice gently over the rice mixture like light raindrops. Use a little salt and pepper to season it according to your preference. Mix everything until all the ingredients are evenly mixed.
4. Take one grape leaf and place it flat on a clean surface, shiny side down. Remove the stem if it's too thick. Add about a tablespoon of the rice filling near the bottom center of the leaf.
5. Take the bottom part of the leaf and cover the filling with it. After that, fold the sides and roll them up tightly to make a nice, round shape. Do the same thing again with the remaining grape leaves and filling.
6. Put the stuffed grape leaves in a big pot with the seam facing downwards. Arrange them closely together in layers.
7. Pour enough water into the pot to cover the stuffed grape leaves. Place a plate upside down on top of the grape leaves to keep them from unraveling during cooking.
8. Put a lid on the pot and heat the water until it bubbles and steam. Turn down the heat and allow the grape leaves to cook slowly for around 25-30 minutes or until the rice is fully cooked and the grape leaves are soft.
9. Remove the stuffed grape leaves from the pot and let them cool slightly before serving.

Nutrition Information (per serving):

- Calories: 550 kcal
- Total Fat: 29g
- Saturated Fat: 4g
- Trans Fat: 0g
- Cholesterol: 0mg
- Sodium: 300mg
- Total Carbohydrate: 67g
- Dietary Fiber: 7g
- Sugars: 2g
- Protein: 10g

ROASTED RED PEPPER AND FETA DIP

Prep Time: 15 minutes Cook Time: 25 minutes Servings: 2

Ingredients:

- 2 large red bell peppers
- 1 cup crumbled feta cheese
- 1/4 cup Greek yogurt
- 2 cloves garlic, minced
- 1 tablespoon extra virgin olive oil
- 1 teaspoon lemon juice
- 1/2 teaspoon dried oregano
- Salt and pepper to taste
- Fresh parsley for garnish
- Pita bread or sliced veggies for serving

Directions:

1. Please turn on your oven and set it to 450 degrees Fahrenheit (230 degrees Celsius). Place a sheet of special paper on a tray that is used for baking.
2. Slice the red bell peppers in the middle and remove the seeds and stems. Place the halves of the pepper on the baking sheet, ensuring the cut side faces down.
3. Put the peppers in the oven and cook them for about 20-25 minutes until the skin becomes burnt and bubbly.
4. Take the cooked peppers out of the oven and immediately put them in a bowl. Cover the bowl with plastic wrap and let the peppers steam for about 10 minutes. This will help in taking off the skins more easily.
5. Peel the skin off the roasted peppers and discard it. Chop the roasted peppers into small pieces.
6. Mix the roasted peppers, feta cheese, Greek yogurt, garlic, olive oil, lemon juice, oregano, salt, and pepper in a blender.
7. Pulse the mixture until smooth and creamy but with some texture remaining.
8. Taste and adjust the seasonings if needed.
9. Put the dip into a bowl for serving and add fresh parsley on top.
10. You can enjoy the Roasted Red Pepper and Feta Dip with pita bread or cut-up vegetables for dipping.

Nutrition Information (per serving):

- Calories: 280 kcal
- Total Fat: 21g
- Saturated Fat: 10g
- Trans Fat: 0g
- Cholesterol: 55mg
- Sodium: 720mg
- Total Carbohydrate: 13g
- Dietary Fiber: 2g
- Sugars: 7g
- Protein: 10g

GRILLED EGGPLANT ROLL-UPS WITH HERBED GOAT CHEESE

Prep Time: 15 minutes Grill Time: 6 minutes Servings: 2

Ingredients:

- 1 large eggplant
- 1 tablespoon olive oil
- 4 ounces goat cheese, softened
- 2 tablespoons fresh basil, finely chopped
- 1 tablespoon fresh parsley, finely chopped
- 1 clove garlic, minced
- Salt and pepper to taste
- Balsamic glaze for drizzling
- Toothpicks

Directions:

1. Preheat your grill to medium-high heat.

2. Cut the eggplant into long thin pieces, around 1/4 inch thick. Put olive oil on both sides of the eggplant slices and sprinkle salt and pepper.
3. Grill the eggplant slices on each side for 2-3 minutes. Take them off the grill and allow them to cool a bit.
4. Mix the creamy goat cheese, chopped basil, parsley, minced garlic, and a small amount of salt and pepper in a small bowl.
5. Lay the grilled eggplant slices on a clean surface. Spread a thin layer of the herbed goat cheese mixture onto each piece.
6. Carefully roll up each eggplant slice to form a roll-up. Secure the roll-ups with toothpicks to keep them in place.
7. Arrange the Grilled Eggplant Roll-Ups with Herbed Goat Cheese on a serving platter.
8. Drizzle the roll-ups with balsamic glaze for added flavor and sweetness.
9. Serve the roll-ups as a delicious appetizer or light lunch to enjoy with your partner.

Nutrition Information (per serving):

- Calories: 260 kcal
- Total Fat: 19g
- Saturated Fat: 10g
- Trans Fat: 0g
- Cholesterol: 35mg
- Sodium: 220mg
- Total Carbohydrate: 15g
- Dietary Fiber: 7g
- Sugars: 8g
- Protein: 11g

MARINATED OLIVES WITH HERBS AND CITRUS

Prep Time: 10 minutes Marinating Time: 2 hours Servings: 2

Ingredients:

- 1 cup mixed olives (such as green and black olives)
- 2 tablespoons extra-virgin olive oil
- 1 teaspoon fresh lemon zest
- 1 teaspoon fresh orange zest
- 1 tablespoon fresh lemon juice
- 1 tablespoon fresh orange juice
- 2 cloves garlic, thinly sliced
- 1 teaspoon dried oregano
- 1 teaspoon dried thyme
- 1 teaspoon dried rosemary
- Pinch of red pepper flakes (optional)

- Fresh herbs like parsley or basil decorate or add flavor to a dish.

Directions:

1. In a medium-sized bowl, combine the mixed olives, extra-virgin olive oil, lemon zest, orange zest, lemon juice, and orange juice. Toss well to coat the olives with citrusy goodness.
2. Add the thinly sliced garlic, dried oregano, dried thyme, dried rosemary, and a pinch of red pepper flakes if you desire some spice. Mix everything to distribute the flavors evenly.
3. Put plastic wrap in the refrigerator bowl for at least 2 hours. This lets the flavors mix with the olives.
4. Before serving, let the olives come to room temperature. Sprinkle parsley or basil on top for a pop of color and fresh taste.
5. Transfer the Marinated Olives with Herbs and Citrus to a serving dish, and they are ready to be enjoyed as a tasty and flavorful appetizer or a delightful side dish.

Nutrition Information (per serving):

- Calories: 140 kcal
- Total Fat: 14g
- Saturated Fat: 2g
- Trans Fat: 0g
- Cholesterol: 0mg
- Sodium: 380mg
- Total Carbohydrate: 4g
- Dietary Fiber: 2g
- Sugars: 0g
- Protein: 1g

TZATZIKI CUCUMBER CUPS

Prep Time: 20 minutes. Servings: 2

Ingredients:

- 2 medium cucumbers
- 1 cup Greek yogurt
- 1/4 cup grated cucumber
- 2 cloves garlic, minced
- 1 tablespoon fresh lemon juice
- 1 tablespoon chopped fresh dill
- 1 tablespoon chopped fresh mint
- Salt and pepper, to taste
- Cherry tomatoes and fresh dill for garnish

Directions:

1. Start by washing the cucumbers and cutting off both ends. To create a striped effect, use a vegetable peeler to remove strips of skin from a vegetable. Make sure to leave some skin on for the desired result. Cut the cucumbers into 1-inch thick slices.
2. You can use either a melon baller or a small spoon to remove the seeds from each slice of cucumber. This will make the cucumber slice have a shape like a cup. Be careful not to dig all the way through.
3. Combine the Greek yogurt, grated cucumber, minced garlic, fresh lemon juice, chopped dill, and chopped mint in a medium-sized bowl. Stir well to incorporate all the flavors. Season with salt and pepper to taste.
4. Fill each cucumber cup with a generous spoonful of the Tzatziki mixture, ensuring the cups are nicely filled.
5. Garnish each cucumber cup with a halved cherry tomato on top and a small sprig of fresh dill for an added burst of color and freshness.
6. Arrange the Tzatziki Cucumber Cups on a serving platter and serve immediately.

Nutrition Information (per serving):

- Calories: 110 kcal
- Total Fat: 4g
- Saturated Fat: 2g
- Trans Fat: 0g
- Cholesterol: 10mg
- Sodium: 50mg
- Total Carbohydrate: 11g
- Dietary Fiber: 2g
- Sugars: 6g
- Protein: 9g

ARTICHOKE AND WHITE BEAN DIP

Prep Time: 15 minutes. Servings: 2

Ingredients:

- 1 can (14 oz) artichoke hearts, drained and chopped
- 1 can (15 oz) white beans, drained and rinsed
- 1/4 cup grated Parmesan cheese
- 1/4 cup Greek yogurt
- 2 cloves garlic, minced
- 2 tablespoons fresh lemon juice
- 2 tablespoons chopped fresh parsley
- 1 tablespoon olive oil
- Salt and pepper, to taste
- Pita bread or vegetable sticks for serving

Directions:

1. Combine the chopped artichoke hearts, white beans, grated Parmesan cheese, Greek yogurt, minced garlic, fresh lemon juice, chopped parsley, and olive oil in a food processor.

2. Pulse the mixture until it reaches a smooth and creamy consistency. You can add a splash of water or more Greek yogurt to achieve the desired texture if needed.
3. Add salt and pepper to the dip until it tastes good. Adjust the seasoning according to your preference.
4. Transfer the Artichoke and White Bean Dip to a serving bowl and drizzle a little olive oil on top for added flavor and shine.
5. Serve the dip with pita bread or vegetable sticks like carrots, celery, and cucumber for a delicious and healthy dipping experience.

Nutrition Information (per serving):

- Calories: 220 kcal
- Total Fat: 6g
- Saturated Fat: 1.5g
- Trans Fat: 0g
- Cholesterol: 5mg
- Sodium: 450mg
- Total Carbohydrate: 32g
- Dietary Fiber: 9g
- Sugars: 2g
- Protein: 13g

LEMON AND HERB ROASTED CHICKPEAS

Prep Time: 10 minutes Cook Time: 20-25 minutes Servings: 2

Ingredients:

- 1 can of chickpeas that weigh 15 ounces. The chickpeas need to be drained and rinsed.
- 2 tablespoons olive oil
- Zest of 1 lemon
- 1 teaspoon dried thyme
- 1 teaspoon dried rosemary
- 1/2 teaspoon garlic powder
- 1/2 teaspoon onion powder
- Salt and pepper, to taste

Directions:

1. Turn your oven to 400 degrees Fahrenheit (or 200 degrees Celsius) and cover a baking sheet with parchment paper.

2. Mix the chickpeas that have been drained and rinsed in a medium-sized bowl with olive oil, lemon peel, dried thyme, rosemary, garlic powder, onion powder, salt, and pepper. Toss the chickpeas until they are evenly coated with the seasoning.
3. Place the spiced chickpeas in a thin layer on the baking sheet.
4. Roast the chickpeas in the oven for about 20-25 minutes or until they become crispy and golden brown. Remember to shake the baking sheet now and then to ensure everything gets evenly roasted.
5. Once the Lemon and Herb Roasted Chickpeas are done, remove them from the oven and let them cool slightly.
6. You can eat the chickpeas as a delicious, crispy snack or put them on top of salads or soups.

Nutrition Information (per serving):

- Calories: 230 kcal
- Total Fat: 10g
- Saturated Fat: 1.5g
- Trans Fat: 0g
- Cholesterol: 0mg
- Sodium: 390mg
- Total Carbohydrate: 27g
- Dietary Fiber: 7g
- Sugars: 2g
- Protein: 8g

CHAPTER 3: SOUPS AND SALADS

GREEK SALAD WITH FETA AND KALAMATA OLIVES

Prep Time: 15 minutes. Servings: 2

Ingredients:

- 2 cups cherry tomatoes, halved
- 1 cucumber, diced
- 1 red bell pepper, diced
- 1/2 red onion, thinly sliced
- 1 cup Kalamata olives, pitted
- 1/2 cup crumbled feta cheese
- 1/4 cup fresh parsley, chopped
- 1/4 cup extra-virgin olive oil

- 2 tablespoons red wine vinegar
- 1 teaspoon dried oregano
- Salt and pepper, to taste

Directions:

1. Combine the halved cherry tomatoes, diced cucumber, red bell pepper, and thinly sliced red onion in a large salad bowl.
2. Add the pitted Kalamata olives to the bowl.
3. Mix the olive oil, red wine vinegar, dried oregano, salt, and pepper in a small bowl to create the dressing.
4. Put the dressing on the vegetables in the salad bowl and mix everything evenly until they have a sauce.
5. Sprinkle the crumbled feta cheese and chopped fresh parsley over the salad.
6. Gently toss the salad again to distribute the feta cheese and parsley throughout.
7. Try the salad and add more salt and pepper if you want more flavor.
8. Serve the Greek Salad with Feta and Kalamata Olives immediately, or refrigerate to let the flavors meld together.

Nutrition Info (per serving):

- Calories: 320
- Total Fat: 26g
- Saturated Fat: 7g
- Cholesterol: 25mg
- Sodium: 650mg
- Total Carbohydrates: 15g
- Dietary Fiber: 4g
- Sugars: 7g
- Protein: 6g

TUSCAN BEAN SOUP

Prep Time: 10 minutes Cook Time: 30 minutes Servings: 2

Ingredients:

- 1 tablespoon olive oil
- 1 small onion, finely chopped
- 2 cloves garlic, minced
- 1 carrot, diced
- 1 celery stalk, diced
- 1 teaspoon dried thyme
- 1 teaspoon dried rosemary
- 1 bay leaf
- 2 cups vegetable broth
- 1 (14 oz) can of diced tomatoes

- 1 (14 oz) can cannellini beans, drained and rinsed
- 1 cup chopped fresh spinach
- Salt and pepper, to taste
- Grated Parmesan cheese (optional for serving)

Directions:

1. Put the olive oil in a big pot or saucepan and heat it to medium. Add the chopped onion, minced garlic, and sauté until the onion becomes translucent.
2. Put the chopped carrot and celery into the pot and cook for a little longer until they become soft.
3. Mix in the dried thyme, rosemary, and bay leaf, and cook for one more minute to let their flavors come out.
4. Pour in the vegetable broth and diced tomatoes with their juice. Heat the soup gently until it starts to bubble slightly, and let it cook for approximately 15-20 minutes so that the flavors can mix.
5. Put the drained and rinsed cannellini beans in the soup and cook them for 5-10 minutes until hot.
6. Stir in the chopped fresh spinach and let it wilt into the soup.
7. Season the Tuscan Bean Soup with salt and pepper to taste.
8. Please take out the bay leaf from the soup before you serve it.
9. If you want to, use a spoon to put the soup into bowls and sprinkle grated Parmesan cheese on top.

Nutrition Info (per serving):

- Calories: 320
- Total Fat: 7g
- Saturated Fat: 1g
- Cholesterol: 0mg
- Sodium: 900mg
- Total Carbohydrates: 54g
- Dietary Fiber: 15g
- Sugars: 8g
- Protein: 16g

CLASSIC MEDITERRANEAN GAZPACHO

Prep Time: 15 minutes Chill Time: 2 hours Servings: 2

Ingredients:

- 4 ripe tomatoes, diced
- 1 cucumber, peeled and diced
- 1 red bell pepper, diced
- 1 small red onion, finely chopped
- 2 cloves garlic, minced
- 3 cups tomato juice
- 2 tablespoons red wine vinegar
- 2 tablespoons extra-virgin olive oil
- 1 teaspoon dried oregano
- 1 teaspoon dried basil
- Salt and pepper, to taste
- Fresh basil leaves for garnish

Directions:

1. Combine the diced tomatoes, cucumber, red bell pepper, red onion, and minced garlic in a big bowl.
2. In a machine like a blender or food processor, blend half of the mixture of tomatoes and cucumbers with the juice from the tomatoes until it becomes a smooth liquid.
3. Put the smooth mixture back into the bowl with the rest of the chopped vegetables.
4. Stir in the red wine vinegar, extra-virgin olive oil, dried oregano, and dried basil. Season with salt and pepper to taste.
5. Put plastic wrap on the bowl and keep the gazpacho in the fridge for at least 2 hours. This will help the flavors mix, and the soup becomes cold.
6. Before serving, give the gazpacho a good stir. If needed, adjust the seasoning with more salt and pepper.
7. Ladle the chilled gazpacho into bowls and garnish with fresh basil leaves.

Nutrition Info (per serving):

- Calories: 190
- Total Fat: 10g
- Saturated Fat: 1.5g
- Cholesterol: 0mg
- Sodium: 660mg
- Total Carbohydrates: 25g
- Dietary Fiber: 5g
- Sugars: 13g
- Protein: 4g

ITALIAN MINESTRONE

Prep Time: 15 minutes Cook Time: 30 minutes Servings: 4

Ingredients:

- 2 tablespoons olive oil
- 1 onion, chopped
- 2 carrots, diced
- 2 celery stalks, diced
- 3 cloves garlic, minced
- 1 can (14 oz) diced tomatoes
- 6 cups vegetable broth
- 1 cup canned cannellini beans, drained and rinsed
- 1 cup chopped zucchini
- 1 cup chopped green beans
- 1 cup chopped cabbage
- 1 cup diced potatoes
- 1 teaspoon dried basil
- 1 teaspoon dried oregano

- 1 bay leaf
- Salt and pepper, to taste
- Use 1 cup of small pasta like macaroni or ditalini.
- Fresh parsley, chopped, for garnish
- Grated Parmesan cheese for serving

Directions:

1. In a big pot, warm the olive oil on medium heat. Put the cut onion, carrots, and celery together. Sauté for about 5 minutes until the vegetables start to soften.
2. Mix in the finely chopped garlic and cook for another minute until it smells pleasant.
3. Add the diced tomatoes, vegetable broth, cannellini beans, zucchini, green beans, cabbage, and diced potatoes to the pot. Stir in the dried basil, oregano, bay leaf, salt, and pepper.
4. Heat the mixture until it boils. Then, lower the heat, put a lid on the pot, and let it cook gently for around 20-25 minutes until the vegetables become soft.
5. In the meantime, cook the small pasta according to the package instructions. Drain and set aside.
6. After cooking the vegetables, put the cooked pasta into the pot and mix them together. Add more salt and pepper to the dish if it needs more flavor.
7. Remove the bay leaf from the soup.
8. Ladle the Italian Minestrone into bowls, garnish with chopped fresh parsley, and serve with grated Parmesan cheese on the side.

Nutrition Info (per serving):

- Calories: 320
- Total Fat: 8g
- Saturated Fat: 1g
- Cholesterol: 0mg
- Sodium: 900mg
- Total Carbohydrates: 53g
- Dietary Fiber: 12g
- Sugars: 10g
- Protein: 12g

MOROCCAN LENTIL SALAD

Prep Time: 10 minutes Cook Time: 20 minutes Servings: 4

Ingredients:

- 1 cup dried lentils
- 2 cups water
- 1 cucumber, diced
- 1 red bell pepper, diced
- 1/2 red onion, finely chopped
- 1/4 cup chopped fresh parsley
- 1/4 cup chopped fresh mint
- 1/3 cup crumbled feta cheese
- 1/4 cup chopped toasted almonds
- 2 tablespoons olive oil
- 2 tablespoons lemon juice
- 1 teaspoon ground cumin
- 1/2 teaspoon ground coriander
- 1/2 teaspoon paprika

- Salt and pepper, to taste

Directions:

1. Rinse the lentils under cold water and drain. In a pot, mix the lentils and water. Bring to a boil over high heat, then turn down the heat to a lower level, put a lid on the pot, and allow the lentils to cook gently for approximately 15 to 20 minutes. Or until they are tender but still hold their shape. Remove any extra water and let the lentils cool.
2. Combine the cooked lentils, diced cucumber, red bell pepper, finely chopped red onion, chopped fresh parsley, and chopped fresh mint in a big bowl.
3. Mix the olive oil, lemon juice, ground cumin, coriander, paprika, salt, and pepper in a small bowl to make the dressing.
4. Pour the dressing over the lentil mixture and toss everything together until well combined.
5. Add the crumbled feta cheese and chopped toasted almonds to the salad. Gently toss to distribute the cheese and almonds evenly.
6. Try the food; add some if it needs more salt and pepper.
7. Serve the Moroccan Lentil Salad immediately or refrigerate for a few hours to let the flavors meld together.

Nutrition Info (per serving):

- Calories: 290
- Total Fat: 14g
- Saturated Fat: 3g
- Cholesterol: 8mg
- Sodium: 245mg
- Total Carbohydrates: 30g
- Dietary Fiber: 12g
- Sugars: 3g
- Protein: 14g

MEDITERRANEAN QUINOA SALAD

Prep Time: 15 minutes Cook Time: 20 minutes Servings: 4

Ingredients:

- 1 cup quinoa, rinsed and drained
- 2 cups water
- 1 cucumber, diced
- 1 red bell pepper, diced
- 1/2 red onion, finely chopped
- 1 cup cherry tomatoes, halved
- 1/2 cup pitted Kalamata olives, sliced
- 1/4 cup crumbled feta cheese
- 1/4 cup chopped fresh parsley
- 1/4 cup chopped fresh mint
- 2 tablespoons extra-virgin olive oil
- 2 tablespoons lemon juice
- 2 cloves garlic, minced

- 1 teaspoon dried oregano
- Salt and pepper, to taste

Directions:

1. In a medium pot, mix the quinoa and water. Heat the saucepan until the water boils. Then, turn down the heat and cover the saucepan. Leave the quinoa to cook for 15-20 minutes until it absorbs the water and becomes fluffy. Remove from heat and let it cool.
2. Combine the cooled quinoa, diced cucumber, red bell pepper, finely chopped red onion, halved cherry tomatoes, and sliced Kalamata olives in a large bowl.
3. Whisk together the extra-virgin olive oil, lemon juice, minced garlic, dried oregano, salt, and pepper in a small bowl to make the dressing.
4. Put the dressing on the quinoa mixture and mix everything until it is blended well.
5. Add the crumbled feta cheese, chopped fresh parsley, and chopped fresh mint to the salad. Gently toss to distribute the cheese and herbs evenly.
6. Try the food and add more salt and pepper if it needs more flavor.
7. Serve the Mediterranean Quinoa Salad immediately or refrigerate for a few hours to let the flavors meld together.

Nutrition Info (per serving):

- Calories: 330
- Total Fat: 15g
- Saturated Fat: 3g
- Cholesterol: 8mg
- Sodium: 250mg
- Total Carbohydrates: 40g
- Dietary Fiber: 8g
- Sugars: 4g
- Protein: 10g

GREEK ORZO SALAD WITH LEMON AND DILL

Prep Time: 15 minutes Cook Time: 10 minutes Chill Time: 30 minutes Servings: 4

Ingredients:

- 1 cup orzo pasta
- 1 cucumber, diced
- 1 cup cherry tomatoes, halved
- 1/2 red onion, finely chopped
- 1/2 cup crumbled feta cheese
- 1/4 cup Kalamata olives, sliced
- 2 tablespoons chopped fresh dill
- Zest and juice of 1 lemon
- 3 tablespoons extra-virgin olive oil
- 1 clove garlic, minced
- Salt and pepper, to taste

Directions:

1. Cook the orzo pasta as directed on the package until it is cooked but still firm. Drain and rinse with cold water to make it cool.
2. Combine the cooked orzo, diced cucumber, halved cherry tomatoes, finely chopped red onion, crumbled feta cheese, and sliced Kalamata olives in a large bowl.
3. Mix the chopped fresh dill, lemon zest, lemon juice, olive oil, minced garlic, salt, and pepper in a little dish to make the dressing.
4. Pour the dressing over the orzo salad and toss everything together until well-coated.
5. Try the food and add more salt and pepper if it doesn't taste flavorful enough.
6. Place the Greek Orzo Salad in the refrigerator for at least 30 minutes to mix the flavors.
7. Before serving, garnish the salad with a sprinkle of fresh dill.

Nutrition Info (per serving):

- Calories: 320
- Total Fat: 14g
- Saturated Fat: 4g
- Cholesterol: 13mg
- Sodium: 220mg
- Total Carbohydrates: 42g
- Dietary Fiber: 3g
- Sugars: 3g
- Protein: 8g

MEDITERRANEAN CHICKPEA SALAD

Prep Time: 15 minutes Chill Time: 30 minutes Servings: 4

Ingredients:

- 1 can (15 ounces) of chickpeas (garbanzo beans), depleted and flushed
- 1 cucumber, diced
- 1 red bell pepper, diced
- 1/2 red onion, finely chopped
- 1 cup cherry tomatoes, halved
- 1/2 container Kalamata olives, set and cut
- 1/4 cup crumbled feta cheese
- 1/4 cup chopped fresh parsley
- 2 tablespoons chopped fresh mint
- 2 tablespoons extra-virgin olive oil
- 1 tablespoon red wine vinegar
- Juice of 1 lemon
- 1 clove garlic, minced
- Salt and pepper, to taste

Directions:

1. Combine the chickpeas, diced cucumber, red bell pepper, finely chopped red onion, halved cherry tomatoes, and sliced Kalamata olives in a large bowl.
2. Whisk together the extra-virgin olive oil, ruddy wine vinegar, lemon juice, minced garlic, salt, and pepper in a separate small bowl to make the dressing.
3. Put the dressing on the chickpea salad and mix everything until it's well-covered.
4. Add the crumbled feta cheese, chopped fresh parsley, and chopped fresh mint to the salad. Gently toss to combine.
5. Try the food and add more salt and pepper if it needs more flavor.
6. Put the Mediterranean Chickpea Salad in the refrigerator for at least 30 minutes to mix the flavors.
7. Before you serve the salad, mix it one last time and add a small piece of fresh mint on top for decoration.

Nutrition Info (per serving):

- Calories: 260
- Total Fat: 12g
- Saturated Fat: 2g
- Cholesterol: 6mg
- Sodium: 420mg
- Total Carbohydrates: 30g
- Dietary Fiber: 8g
- Sugars: 6g
- Protein: 8g

TUSCAN PANZANELLA SALAD

Prep Time: 20 minutes Resting Time: 15 minutes Servings: 4

Ingredients:

- 4 cups stale bread (preferably Italian or French), cut into bite-sized cubes
- 2 cups ripe tomatoes, diced
- 1 cucumber, sliced
- 1/2 red onion, thinly sliced
- Half a cup of Kalamata olives that have had the pits removed and cut in half.
- 1/4 cup capers, drained
- 1/2 cup fresh basil leaves, torn
- 1/4 cup fresh parsley, chopped
- 1/4 cup extra-virgin olive oil
- 2 tablespoons red wine vinegar
- 2 cloves garlic, minced
- Salt and pepper, to taste

Directions:

1. Combine the stale bread cubes, diced tomatoes, cucumber slices, thinly sliced red onion, halved Kalamata olives, and drained capers in a large bowl.
2. Mix the olive oil, red wine vinegar, minced garlic, salt, and pepper in a small bowl to make the dressing.
3. Drizzle the dressing over the bread and vegetable mixture in a large bowl. Gently toss everything together until the bread is coated with the sauce.
4. Let the Panzanella Salad sit for about 15 minutes so that the flavors can mix well.
5. Add the torn basil leaves and chopped fresh parsley to the salad before serving. Toss gently to combine.
6. Try the food and add more salt and pepper if you want it to have more flavor.
7. Serve the Tuscan Panzanella Salad in individual bowls or on a platter. Garnish with extra basil leaves for a fresh and inviting presentation.

Nutrition Info (per serving):

- Calories: 320
- Total Fat: 17g
- Saturated Fat: 2g
- Cholesterol: 0mg
- Sodium: 490mg
- Total Carbohydrates: 37g
- Dietary Fiber: 5g
- Sugars: 5g
- Protein: 6g

GREEK AVGOLEMONO SOUP

Prep Time: 10 minutes Cook Time: 15 minutes Servings: 4

Ingredients:

- 4 cups chicken broth
- 1/2 cup orzo pasta
- 3 large eggs
- 1/4 cup fresh lemon juice
- 1 cup cooked chicken, shredded
- Salt and pepper, to taste
- Fresh dill, for garnish (optional)

Directions:

1. Heat the chicken broth on medium heat until it simmers gently in a big saucepan.

2. Put the orzo pasta in the simmering broth and cook it until it is firm but not too soft, following the instructions on the package.
3. While the orzo is boiling, mix the eggs and lemon juice in a different bowl until well blended.
4. Once the orzo is cooked, reduce the heat to low. Slowly add a ladleful of the hot broth into the egg-lemon mixture while whisking continuously. This step is crucial to temper the eggs and prevent curdling.
5. Gradually pour the tempered egg-lemon mixture back into the saucepan with the orzo and chicken broth, stirring gently to combine.
6. Stir in the shredded cooked chicken and let the soup simmer for a few more minutes until slightly thickened.
7. Season the Avgolemono Soup with salt and pepper to taste.
8. Serve the Greek Avgolemono Soup hot, garnished with fresh dill if desired.

Nutrition Info (per serving):

- Calories: 250
- Total Fat: 9g
- Saturated Fat: 2g
- Cholesterol: 180mg
- Sodium: 900mg
- Total Carbohydrates: 19g
- Dietary Fiber: 1g
- Sugars: 1g
- Protein: 21g

CHAPTER 4: MAIN DISH RECIPES

MEDITERRANEAN GRILLED CHICKEN WITH LEMON AND GARLIC

Prep Time: 40 minutes (including marinating time). Cook Time: 15 minutes. Servings: 2

Ingredients:

- 2 boneless, skinless chicken breasts
- 1/4 cup extra-virgin olive oil
- 3 cloves garlic, minced
- 1 lemon, juiced and zested
- 1 teaspoon dried oregano
- 1 teaspoon dried thyme
- 1/2 teaspoon dried rosemary
- Salt and pepper, to taste
- Fresh parsley, for garnish (optional)
- Lemon wedges for serving

Directions:

1. Mix the olive oil, minced garlic, lemon juice, lemon zest, dried oregano, dried thyme, and rosemary in a bowl. Season with salt and pepper to taste.
2. Put the chicken breasts in a not-deep container and pour the sauce. Make sure the chicken has a good amount of covering on it. Put a lid on the dish and put it in the fridge for 30 minutes. This will let the flavors mix into the chicken.
3. Preheat the grill to medium-high heat. Take the chicken out of the marinade and gently shake off any extra.
4. Cook the chicken on both sides for around 7 minutes or until the inside of the chicken is 165°F (74°C) and there is no pink color in the middle.
5. Take the grilled chicken off the heat and allow it to sit briefly before cutting it into slices.
6. Add some fresh parsley on top, and give lemon wedges on the side for more taste.

Nutrition Info (per serving):

- Calories: 320
- Total Fat: 18g
- Saturated Fat: 3g
- Cholesterol: 80mg
- Sodium: 160mg
- Total Carbohydrates: 3g
- Dietary Fiber: 1g
- Sugars: 1g
- Protein: 35g

MOROCCAN SPICED LAMB KEBABS

Prep Time: 1 hour (including marinating time) Cook Time: 10 minutes Servings: 2-3

Ingredients:

- 1 lb (450g) lamb leg or shoulder, cut into bite-sized pieces
- 2 tablespoons olive oil
- 2 cloves garlic, minced
- 1 teaspoon ground cumin
- 1 teaspoon ground coriander
- 1/2 teaspoon ground paprika
- 1/2 teaspoon ground cinnamon
- 1/4 teaspoon ground ginger
- 1/4 teaspoon ground turmeric
- 1/4 teaspoon cayenne pepper (optional for heat)
- Salt and pepper, to taste
- 1 lemon, juiced
- Fresh cilantro or parsley for garnish (optional)

Directions:

1. In a big bowl, combine olive oil, minced garlic, cumin, coriander, paprika, cinnamon, ginger, turmeric, cayenne pepper (if you want it spicy), and a little salt and pepper.
2. Put the small pieces of lamb in the bowl and mix them well to cover the meat evenly with the spices. Cover the bowl and let it marinate in the refrigerator for at least 1 hour, ideally overnight, to allow the flavors to meld.
3. If you use wooden skewers, put them in water for around 30 minutes to avoid them getting burnt when you put them on the grill.
4. Preheat the grill to medium-high heat. Thread the marinated lamb pieces onto the skewers, leaving a little space between each piece.
5. Cook the lamb kebabs on a grill for around 8-10 minutes, flipping them sometimes. Keep cooking until they are done how you like them and have a nice burnt part on the sides.
6. Once the kebabs are done, remove them from the grill and drizzle fresh lemon juice.
7. Put some cut cilantro or parsley on the surface, and serve the Moroccan Spiced Lamb Kebabs while still hot. You can enjoy them with side dishes such as couscous, roasted vegetables, or a fresh salad.

Nutrition Info (per serving, for 2 servings):

- Calories: 450
- Total Fat: 30g
- Saturated Fat: 10g
- Cholesterol: 125mg
- Sodium: 90mg
- Total Carbohydrates: 2g
- Dietary Fiber: 1g
- Sugars: 0g
- Protein: 40g

GREEK LEMON AND HERB SALMON

Prep Time: 10 minutes (plus marinating time). Cook Time: 15-20 minutes Servings: 2

Ingredients:

- 2 salmon fillets
- 2 tablespoons olive oil
- 2 cloves garlic, minced
- Zest of 1 lemon
- Juice of 1 lemon
- 1 teaspoon dried oregano
- 1 teaspoon dried thyme
- 1/2 teaspoon dried rosemary
- 1/2 teaspoon dried dill
- Salt and pepper, to taste
- Fresh parsley, for garnish (optional)
- Lemon wedges for serving

Directions:

1. Turn on the oven and set it to 375°F (190°C). Put the material paper on a preparing sheet or include a little sum of oil in it.
2. Mix the olive oil, minced garlic, lemon zest, lemon juice, dried oregano, dried thyme, rosemary, dill, salt, and pepper in a small bowl.
3. Put the pieces of salmon on the baking sheet that has been prepared. Drizzle the lemon and herb mixture onto the salmon, covering each piece evenly.
4. Let the salmon marinate in the lemon and herb mixture for 15-20 minutes, allowing the flavors to infuse the fish.
5. After you soak the salmon in a special sauce, put it in a pan and cook it in the oven for about 15-20 minutes until it is ready and easily broken apart with a fork.
6. Take the salmon out of the oven and add fresh parsley on top if you want to. Serve the Greek Lemon and Herb Salmon hot with lemon wedges on the side.

Nutrition Info (per serving, for 2 servings):

- Calories: 350
- Total Fat: 22g
- Saturated Fat: 3.5g
- Cholesterol: 95mg
- Sodium: 150mg
- Total Carbohydrates: 2g
- Dietary Fiber: 0g
- Sugars: 0g
- Protein: 34g

ITALIAN EGGPLANT PARMESAN

Prep Time: 30 minutes Cook Time: 20-25 minutes Servings: 4-6

Ingredients:

- 2 large eggplants, sliced into 1/4-inch thick rounds
- 2 cups marinara sauce
- 2 cups shredded mozzarella cheese
- 1 cup grated Parmesan cheese
- 1 cup all-purpose flour
- 3 large eggs, beaten
- 2 cups Italian-style breadcrumbs
- 1 teaspoon dried oregano
- 1 teaspoon dried basil
- 1/2 teaspoon garlic powder
- Salt and pepper, to taste
- Olive oil for frying
- Fresh basil leaves, for garnish (optional)

Directions:

1. Preheat the oven to 375°F (190°C). Gently coat a baking dish with olive oil or non-stick cooking spray.
2. In a shallow dish, mix the Italian-style breadcrumbs with dried oregano, dried basil, garlic powder, salt, and pepper.
3. Set up a breading station: place the all-purpose flour in one dish, the beaten eggs in another container, and the breadcrumb mixture in a third dish.
4. Dredge each eggplant slice in flour, shaking off any excess. Then dip the eggplant slice into the beaten eggs, ensuring it is evenly coated. Lastly, push the eggplant slice into the breadcrumb mixture, ensuring it is completely covered on both sides.
5. In a big pan, warm up some olive oil on medium heat to fry the eggplant slices. Fry the breaded eggplant slices in batches for 2-3 minutes per side or until golden brown and crispy. Place the fried eggplant slices on a paper towel-lined plate to absorb excess oil.
6. In the prepared baking dish, spread a thin layer of marinara sauce. Place a layer of cooked eggplant slices on top of the sauce. Sprinkle some shredded mozzarella and grated Parmesan cheese over the eggplant. Keep adding layers of ingredients until they're all used, and end with a layer of cheese on top.
7. Bake the Italian Eggplant Parmesan in the oven for 20-25 minutes or until the cheese is bubbly and lightly browned.
8. Take the food out of the oven and wait for it to cool down before you start eating. Garnish with fresh basil leaves, if desired.

Nutrition Info (per serving, for 4 servings):

- Calories: 420
- Total Fat: 18g
- Saturated Fat: 7g
- Cholesterol: 126mg
- Sodium: 1047mg
- Total Carbohydrates: 45g
- Dietary Fiber: 8g
- Sugars: 11g
- Protein: 22g

SPANISH PAELLA WITH SEAFOOD AND SAFFRON

Prep Time: 15 minutes Cook Time: 35 minutes Servings: 4-6

Ingredients:

- 1 cup Arborio rice (or short-grain rice)
- 1 lb mixed seafood (shrimp, mussels, clams, calamari, etc.)
- 1 onion, finely chopped
- 3 cloves garlic, minced
- 1 red bell pepper, diced
- 1 yellow bell pepper, diced
- 1 cup frozen peas
- 2 tomatoes, diced
- 4 cups seafood or chicken broth
- 1/2 teaspoon saffron threads
- 1/2 teaspoon smoked paprika
- 1/4 teaspoon cayenne pepper (optional for extra spice)
- 1/4 cup dry white wine

- 2 tablespoons olive oil
- Salt and pepper to taste
- Lemon wedges and fresh parsley for garnish

Directions:

1. In a small bowl, crush the saffron threads with your fingers and then soak them in 2 tablespoons of warm water to release their flavor and color.
2. Put the olive oil in a big pan or a shallow skillet and heat it over medium heat. Put the cut onion in and cook it until it becomes softer, for about 2-3 minutes. Put the chopped garlic in the pan and cook it for 30 seconds more.
3. Put the chopped red and yellow bell peppers in the pan and cook until they become soft, which should take around 3-4 minutes.
4. Stir in the Arborio rice, smoked paprika, and cayenne pepper (if using). Cook for 1-2 minutes, stirring constantly, until the rice is well coated in the spices and starts to toast slightly.
5. Put the dry white wine into the dish and allow the rice to absorb most of it while cooking.
6. Add the diced tomatoes, frozen peas, and soaked saffron threads (with the soaking water) to the pan—season with salt and pepper to taste.
7. Pour the seafood or chicken broth and bring the mixture to a simmer. Reduce the heat to low, cover the pan, and let the rice cook for about 15-20 minutes or until the liquid is absorbed and the rice is tender.
8. While the rice is cooking, prepare the seafood. Clean and devein the shrimp if needed. Scrub and rinse the mussels and clams under cold water.
9. Once the rice is done, place the seafood on the rice. Spread the shrimp, calamari, mussels, and clams evenly on the paella. Put the lid back on the pan and wait 5-7 minutes. Check if the shrimp are pink and cooked and if the mussels and clams have opened up.
10. Take the paella off the heat and give it time to cool down before serving it. Add lemon wedges and fresh parsley on top as decoration.

Nutrition Info (per serving, for 4 servings):

- Calories: 480
- Total Fat: 10g
- Saturated Fat: 1.5g

- Cholesterol: 150mg
- Sodium: 850mg
- Total Carbohydrates: 64g
- Dietary Fiber: 5g
- Sugars: 6g
- Protein: 30g

GREEK MOUSSAKA

Prep Time: 30 minutes Cook Time: 1-hour Servings: 4-6

Ingredients:

- 1 large eggplant, sliced into 1/4-inch rounds
- 1 lb ground lamb or beef
- 1 onion, finely chopped
- 3 cloves garlic, minced
- 1 can (14 oz) diced tomatoes
- 1/4 cup tomato paste
- 1 teaspoon dried oregano
- 1/2 teaspoon ground cinnamon
- 1/4 teaspoon ground nutmeg
- 1/4 teaspoon cayenne pepper (optional, for a bit of spice)
- 1/2 cup red wine
- 1/2 cup beef or vegetable broth
- 2 tablespoons olive oil

- Salt and pepper to taste
- 1 cup grated Parmesan or Pecorino cheese

<u>Bechamel sauce:</u>

- 4 tablespoons butter
- 1/4 cup all-purpose flour
- 2 cups milk
- Pinch of ground nutmeg
- Salt and pepper to taste
- 2 large eggs, lightly beaten

Directions:

1. Turn on the oven and set it to 375 degrees Fahrenheit (or 190 degrees Celsius). Put olive oil on a big baking dish and keep it to the side.
2. Place the eggplant slices in a colander and sprinkle them with salt. Let them sit for about 30 minutes to draw out excess moisture. Wash the eggplant slices with cold water and dry them with paper towels.
3. Warm up oil on medium heat in a big pan. Put the ground lamb or beef in a big frying pan and cook it until it turns brown. Take the meat out of the skillet and put it aside.
4. Add another tablespoon of olive oil in the same skillet and sauté the chopped onion until softened. Mix the finely chopped garlic into the pan and continue cooking for 30 more seconds.
5. Return the cooked meat to the skillet and add the diced tomatoes, tomato paste, dried oregano, ground cinnamon, ground nutmeg, cayenne pepper (if using), red wine, and beef or vegetable broth—season with salt and pepper to taste. Simmer the mixture over medium-low heat for 15-20 minutes or until the sauce thickens.
6. In a separate saucepan, prepare the bechamel sauce. Heat the butter on medium until it becomes liquid, then mix in the flour until it becomes a smooth paste. Add the milk little by little while whisking. Keep cooking until the sauce becomes thick and creamy. Stir in a pinch of ground nutmeg, salt, and pepper. Remove the saucepan from the heat and let the sauce cool slightly. Beat in the lightly beaten eggs.
7. To assemble the moussaka, layer half of the eggplant slices in the bottom of the greased baking dish. Top with half the meat sauce and sprinkle half. Do the layers again, but make sure the last layer is cheese.

8. Pour the prepared bechamel sauce over the top layer of cheese, ensuring it covers the entire surface.
9. Cook the moussaka in the oven for around 45 minutes to an hour until the top becomes a nice golden brown and starts to bubble.
10. Take the moussaka out of the oven and wait before cutting and serving it.

Nutrition Info (per serving, for 4 servings):

- Calories: 550
- Total Fat: 35g
- Saturated Fat: 15g
- Cholesterol: 160mg
- Sodium: 690mg
- Total Carbohydrates: 23g
- Dietary Fiber: 5g
- Sugars: 8g
- Protein: 32g

MOROCCAN COUSCOUS WITH VEGETABLES AND CHICKPEAS

Prep Time: 15 minutes Cook Time: 20 minutes Servings: 2-4

Ingredients:

- 1 cup couscous
- 1 1/2 cups vegetable broth or water
- 1 tablespoon olive oil
- 1 onion, chopped
- 2 cloves garlic, minced
- 1 red bell pepper, diced
- 1 zucchini, diced
- 1 carrot, diced
- 1 cup cooked chickpeas (canned or cooked from dry)
- 1 teaspoon ground cumin
- 1/2 teaspoon ground coriander
- 1/2 teaspoon ground cinnamon
- 1/4 teaspoon ground turmeric
- 1/4 teaspoon cayenne pepper (optional, for a bit of heat)

- Salt and pepper to taste
- 1/4 cup chopped fresh parsley
- 1/4 cup chopped fresh cilantro
- Lemon wedges for serving

Directions:

1. Heat the vegetable broth or water in a pot until it boils. Stir in the couscous, cover the saucepan with a lid, and remove it from the heat. Let it sit for about 5 minutes to allow the couscous to absorb the liquid. Fluff the couscous with a fork.
2. Warm up the olive oil on medium heat in a big frying pan. Put the chopped onion in and cook it until it turns see-through.
3. Stir in the minced garlic, diced red bell pepper, diced zucchini, and diced carrot. Cook the vegetables for about 5 minutes or until they start to soften.
4. Add the cooked chickpeas, ground cumin, ground coriander, ground cinnamon, ground turmeric, and cayenne pepper (if using) to the skillet—season with salt and pepper to taste. Stir well to coat the vegetables and chickpeas with the aromatic spices.
5. Cook the mixture for 5-7 minutes or until all the vegetables are tender.
6. Add the cooked couscous to the skillet once the vegetables and chickpeas are cooked. Toss everything together until well combined.
7. Stir in the chopped fresh parsley and cilantro, reserving some for garnish.
8. Serve the Moroccan couscous in individual bowls, garnished with the remaining fresh herbs. Squeeze a wedge of lemon over each serving for an extra citrusy flavor.

Nutrition Info (per serving, for 4 servings):

- Calories: 290
- Total Fat: 6g
- Saturated Fat: 1g
- Cholesterol: 0mg
- Sodium: 240mg
- Total Carbohydrates: 50g
- Dietary Fiber: 9g
- Sugars: 6g
- Protein: 10g

ITALIAN STUFFED BELL PEPPERS

Prep Time: 20 minutes Cook Time: 40 minutes Servings: 4

Ingredients:

- 4 large bell peppers (any color), tops removed and seeds removed
- 1 cup cooked brown rice or quinoa
- 1 tablespoon olive oil
- 1 small onion, finely chopped
- 2 cloves garlic, minced
- 1 pound lean ground turkey or chicken (or use plant-based ground meat for a vegetarian option)
- 1 cup diced tomatoes (canned or fresh)
- 1 teaspoon dried oregano
- 1 teaspoon dried basil
- 1/2 teaspoon dried thyme
- 1/4 teaspoon red pepper flakes (optional, for a bit of heat)
- Salt and pepper to taste
- 1 cup shredded mozzarella cheese (or dairy-free cheese for a vegan option)
- Fresh basil leaves for garnish

Directions:

1. Preheat the oven to 375°F (190°C). Lightly grease a baking dish.
2. In a large pot of boiling water, blanch the bell peppers for 2-3 minutes until slightly softened. Drain and set aside.
3. In a skillet, heat the olive oil over medium heat. Add the chopped onion and sauté until it becomes translucent.
4. Stir in the minced garlic and cook for another minute until fragrant.
5. Add the ground turkey or chicken to the skillet until browned and cooked. If using plant-based ground meat, cook until heated through.
6. Stir in the diced tomatoes, dried oregano, dried basil, dried thyme, red pepper flakes (if using), salt, and pepper. Cook the mixture for 2-3 minutes to allow the flavors to meld.
7. Remove the skillet from heat and stir in the brown rice or quinoa. Mix everything until well combined.
8. Stuff each bell pepper with the turkey (or plant-based) and rice mixture. Press the filling down gently to pack it inside the peppers.
9. Place the stuffed bell peppers in the prepared baking dish. Cover the dish with aluminum foil.
10. Bake in the oven for 25-30 minutes or until the bell peppers are tender.
11. Remove the foil and sprinkle the shredded mozzarella cheese (or dairy-free cheese) over the tops of the stuffed peppers.
12. Return the baking dish to the oven and bake for 5-7 minutes or until the cheese is melted and bubbly.
13. Remove the stuffed bell peppers from the oven and let them cool slightly.
14. Garnish with fresh basil leaves before serving.

Nutrition Info (per serving):

- Calories: 350
- Total Fat: 15g
- Saturated Fat: 5g
- Cholesterol: 85mg
- Sodium: 300mg
- Total Carbohydrates: 20g
- Dietary Fiber: 4g
- Sugars: 6g
- Protein: 35g

SPANISH CHORIZO AND SHRIMP SKEWERS

Prep Time: 20 minutes Marinating Time: 15 minutes Cook Time: 8 minutes Servings: 4

Ingredients:

- 1/2 pound large shrimp, peeled and deveined
- 1/2 pound Spanish chorizo sausage, cut into bite-sized pieces
- 1 red bell pepper, cut into chunks
- 1 green bell pepper, cut into chunks
- 1 red onion, cut into chunks
- 2 tablespoons olive oil
- 2 cloves garlic, minced
- 1 teaspoon smoked paprika
- 1/2 teaspoon ground cumin
- 1/2 teaspoon dried oregano
- Salt and pepper to taste
- Wooden skewers, soaked in water for 30 minutes

Directions:

1. Combine the shrimp, chorizo, bell peppers, and red onion in a large bowl.
2. Mix the olive oil, minced garlic, smoked paprika, ground cumin, dried oregano, salt, and pepper in a separate bowl.
3. Pour the olive oil mixture over the shrimp, chorizo, and vegetables. Toss everything together until well coated. Allow the mixture to marinate for at least 15 minutes to enhance the flavors.
4. Preheat your grill or grill pan over medium-high heat.
5. Thread the marinated shrimp, chorizo, bell peppers, and red onion onto the soaked wooden skewers, alternating the ingredients.
6. Grill the skewers for 3-4 minutes per side or until the shrimp are cooked, and the chorizo is slightly charred.
7. Remove the skewers from the grill and serve immediately.

Nutrition Info (per serving):

- Calories: 350
- Total Fat: 24g
- Saturated Fat: 7g
- Cholesterol: 160mg
- Sodium: 800mg
- Total Carbohydrates: 10g
- Dietary Fiber: 2g
- Sugars: 4g
- Protein: 23g

GREEK SPINACH AND FETA STUFFED CHICKEN

Prep Time: 20 minutes Cook Time: 25 minutes Servings: 4

Ingredients:

- 4 boneless, skinless chicken breasts
- 1 cup fresh spinach leaves
- 1/2 cup crumbled feta cheese
- 1/4 cup sun-dried tomatoes, chopped
- 2 cloves garlic, minced
- 1 tablespoon olive oil
- 1 teaspoon dried oregano
- 1/2 teaspoon dried thyme
- Salt and pepper to taste
- Toothpicks or kitchen twine for securing

Directions:

1. Preheat your oven to 375°F (190°C).
2. Using a sharp knife, carefully slice a pocket into each chicken breast, careful not to cut all the way through.
3. Mix the fresh spinach, crumbled feta cheese, chopped sun-dried tomatoes, minced garlic, olive oil, dried oregano, dried thyme, salt, and pepper in a medium bowl.
4. Stuff each chicken breast with the spinach and feta mixture, pressing it in firmly.
5. Secure the openings of the chicken breasts with toothpicks or tie them with kitchen twine to keep the stuffing in place.
6. Heat a large oven-safe skillet over medium-high heat. Add a little olive oil to the pan if needed.
7. Sear the stuffed chicken breasts in the skillet for 2-3 minutes per side or until they develop a golden-brown crust.
8. Transfer the skillet to the preheated oven and bake for about 15-20 minutes or until the chicken is cooked and reaches an internal temperature of 165°F (74°C).
9. Remove the chicken from the oven and let it rest for a few minutes before serving.
10. Serve the Greek Spinach and Feta Stuffed Chicken with your favorite Mediterranean sides, such as Greek salad, roasted vegetables, or couscous.

Nutrition Info (per serving):

- Calories: 280
- Total Fat: 11g
- Saturated Fat: 4g
- Cholesterol: 100mg
- Sodium: 400mg
- Total Carbohydrates: 4g
- Dietary Fiber: 1g
- Sugars: 1g
- Protein: 38g

CHAPTER 5: SIDE DISHES

ITALIAN ROASTED VEGETABLES WITH BALSAMIC GLAZE

Prep Time: 15 minutes Cook Time: 25-30 minutes Servings: 4

Ingredients:

- 2 cups cherry tomatoes
- 2 cups zucchini, sliced
- 2 cups bell peppers (red, yellow, or orange), sliced
- 1 red onion, cut into wedges
- 1 cup baby carrots
- 4 cloves garlic, minced
- 3 tablespoons olive oil
- 2 tablespoons balsamic vinegar
- 1 teaspoon dried oregano
- 1 teaspoon dried basil
- Salt and pepper to taste
- Fresh basil leaves for garnish

Directions:

1. Preheat your oven to 425°F (220°C). Line a large baking sheet with parchment paper or lightly grease it.
2. Combine the cherry tomatoes, zucchini, bell peppers, red onion, baby carrots, and minced garlic in a large mixing bowl.
3. Drizzle the olive oil and balsamic vinegar over the vegetables. Sprinkle the dried oregano, basil, salt, and pepper on top.
4. Toss the vegetables until they are evenly coated with the oil, vinegar, and seasonings.
5. Spread the vegetables out in a single layer on the prepared baking sheet.
6. Roast the vegetables in the preheated oven for about 25-30 minutes or until they are tender and slightly caramelized, stirring once halfway through cooking.
7. Remove the baking sheet from the oven and drizzle some additional balsamic glaze over the roasted vegetables if desired.
8. Garnish with fresh basil leaves before serving.

Nutrition Info (per serving):

- Calories: 180
- Total Fat: 9g
- Saturated Fat: 1g
- Cholesterol: 0mg
- Sodium: 100mg
- Total Carbohydrates: 23g
- Dietary Fiber: 6g
- Sugars: 12g
- Protein: 4g

GREEK LEMON POTATOES

Prep Time: 15 minutes Cook Time: 55-60 minutes Servings: 4

Ingredients:

- 4 large russet potatoes, peeled and cut into wedges
- 1/4 cup olive oil
- 1/4 cup fresh lemon juice
- 1 teaspoon dried oregano
- 1 teaspoon dried thyme
- 4 garlic cloves, minced
- 1/2 teaspoon salt
- 1/4 teaspoon black pepper
- 1/2 cup vegetable broth or chicken broth
- 1/4 cup water
- Fresh parsley, chopped (for garnish)

Directions:

1. Preheat your oven to 400°F (200°C).

2. Combine the olive oil, lemon juice, dried oregano, dried thyme, minced garlic, salt, and black pepper in a large mixing bowl. Mix well to create the marinade.
3. Add the potato wedges to the bowl with the marinade and toss until the potatoes are evenly coated.
4. Transfer the marinated potatoes to a large baking dish or roasting pan, arranging them in a single layer.
5. Mix the vegetable broth and water in a separate bowl, then pour the mixture into the baking dish around the potatoes.
6. Cover the baking dish with aluminum foil and bake in the oven for about 30 minutes.
7. After 30 minutes, remove the foil and continue baking for 25-30 minutes or until the potatoes are tender and golden brown, turning them once halfway through cooking.
8. Once the potatoes are done, garnish with freshly chopped parsley before serving.

Nutrition Info (per serving):

- Calories: 260
- Total Fat: 11g
- Saturated Fat: 1.5g
- Cholesterol: 0mg
- Sodium: 320mg
- Total Carbohydrates: 36g
- Dietary Fiber: 4g
- Sugars: 2g
- Protein: 4g

MEDITERRANEAN QUINOA PILAF

Prep Time: 10 minutes Cook Time: 20 minutes Servings: 4

Ingredients:

- 1 cup quinoa, rinsed and drained
- 2 cups vegetable broth or water
- 1 tablespoon olive oil
- 1 small onion, finely chopped
- 2 garlic cloves, minced
- 1 red bell pepper, diced
- 1 zucchini, diced
- 1 cup cherry tomatoes, halved
- 1/4 cup Kalamata olives, pitted and sliced
- 2 tablespoons fresh lemon juice
- 1 teaspoon dried oregano
- 1/2 teaspoon dried thyme

- Salt and pepper to taste
- Fresh parsley, chopped (for garnish)

Directions:

1. Combine the flushed quinoa and vegetable broth (or water) in a medium pan. Bring to a boil over medium-high heat. Once boiling, reduce the heat to low, cover the saucepan, and let the quinoa simmer for about 15 minutes or until all the liquid is absorbed and the quinoa is tender.
2. In a partitioned huge skillet, warm the olive oil over medium warm. Add the chopped onion and sauté for 2-3 minutes until softened.
3. Stir in the minced garlic, red bell pepper, and zucchini. Cook for an additional 5-6 minutes until the vegetables are tender.
4. Add the halved cherry tomatoes and sliced Kalamata olives to the skillet. Cook for another 2 minutes until the tomatoes are somewhat mollified.
5. Whisk together the new lemon juice, dried oregano, dried thyme, salt, and pepper in a little bowl.
6. Add the cooked quinoa to the skillet with the sautéed vegetables. Pour the lemon juice mixture over the quinoa and vegetables, tossing everything together until well combined.
7. Remove the skillet from the heat. Taste and adjust the seasonings if needed.
8. Garnish with freshly chopped parsley before serving.

Nutrition Info (per serving):

- Calories: 250
- Total Fat: 8g
- Saturated Fat: 1g
- Cholesterol: 0mg
- Sodium: 380mg
- Total Carbohydrates: 38g
- Dietary Fiber: 7g
- Sugars: 5g
- Protein: 8g

MOROCCAN COUSCOUS WITH ALMONDS AND RAISINS

Prep Time: 10 minutes Cook Time: 15 minutes Servings: 4

Ingredients:

- 1 cup couscous
- 1 1/4 cups vegetable broth or water
- 2 tablespoons olive oil
- 1 small onion, finely chopped
- 2 garlic cloves, minced
- 1 teaspoon ground cumin
- 1/2 teaspoon ground cinnamon
- 1/4 teaspoon ground ginger
- 1/4 teaspoon ground turmeric
- 1/4 teaspoon ground coriander
- Salt and pepper to taste
- 1/4 cup raisins
- 1/4 cup slivered almonds, toasted

- Fresh parsley, chopped (for garnish)

Directions:

1. Bring the vegetable broth (or water) to a bubble in a medium pot. Evacuate from warm, include the couscous, cover the pool, and let it sit for 5 minutes or until it retains the fluid and becomes soft.
2. In an expansive skillet, warm the olive oil over medium warm. Include the chopped onion and sauté for 2-3 minutes until relaxed. Stir in the minced garlic, ground cumin, cinnamon, ginger, turmeric, coriander, salt, and pepper. Cook for an additional 1-2 minutes until the spices become fragrant.
3. Add the cooked couscous with a fork to the skillet with the sautéed onions and spices. Mix everything until well combined.
4. Fold in the raisins and toasted slivered almonds into the couscous mixture.
5. Remove the skillet from the heat. Taste and adjust the seasonings if needed.
6. Garnish with freshly chopped parsley before serving.

Nutrition Info (per serving):

- Calories: 270
- Total Fat: 9g
- Saturated Fat: 1g
- Cholesterol: 0mg
- Sodium: 310mg
- Total Carbohydrates: 41g
- Dietary Fiber: 3g
- Sugars: 7g
- Protein: 6g

ITALIAN CAPRESE SALAD

Prep Time: 10 minutes. Servings: 2

Ingredients:

- 2 large ripe tomatoes, sliced
- 8 ounces fresh mozzarella cheese, sliced
- Fresh basil leaves
- Extra virgin olive oil
- Balsamic glaze
- Salt and pepper to taste

Directions:

1. Arrange the tomato and mozzarella slices alternately on a serving plate.
2. Tuck new basil takes off between the tomato and mozzarella cuts.
3. Sprinkle additional virgin olive oil over the serving of mixed greens.
4. Drizzle balsamic glaze over the top for added sweetness and tanginess.
5. Season with a pinch of salt and freshly ground black pepper.

6. Serve immediately and enjoy this classic Italian salad's fresh and vibrant flavors.

Nutrition Info (per serving):

- Calories: 300
- Total Fat: 21g
- Saturated Fat: 10g
- Cholesterol: 50mg
- Sodium: 450mg
- Total Carbohydrates: 8g
- Dietary Fiber: 2g
- Sugars: 5g
- Protein: 19g

GREEK LEMON AND OREGANO ROASTED ASPARAGUS

Prep Time: 10 minutes Cook Time: 12-15 minutes Servings: 2

Ingredients:

- 1 bunch of fresh asparagus spears
- 2 tablespoons olive oil
- 1 tablespoon fresh lemon juice
- 1 teaspoon dried oregano
- Zest of 1 lemon
- Salt and pepper to taste
- Crumbled feta cheese (optional for serving)

Directions:

1. Preheat your oven to 425°F (220°C). Line a baking sheet with parchment paper.
2. Trim the tough ends of the asparagus spears, and arrange them in a single layer on the prepared baking sheet.
3. Whisk together the olive oil, lemon juice, dried oregano, and lemon zest in a small bowl.

4. Drizzle the lemon and oregano mixture over the asparagus, ensuring each spear is evenly coated.
5. Season the asparagus with salt and pepper to taste.
6. Roast the asparagus in the oven for 12-15 minutes or until tender but still crisp.
7. Remove the roasted asparagus from the oven and transfer them to a serving platter.
8. Optional: Sprinkle crumbled feta cheese over the roasted asparagus for extra flavor.
9. Serve the Greek Lemon and Oregano Roasted Asparagus as a delicious and healthy side dish alongside your favorite Mediterranean-inspired meal.

Nutrition Info (per serving):

- Calories: 120
- Total Fat: 10g
- Saturated Fat: 1.5g
- Cholesterol: 0mg
- Sodium: 5mg
- Total Carbohydrates: 6g
- Dietary Fiber: 3g
- Sugars: 2g
- Protein: 3g

SPANISH GARLIC MUSHROOMS

Prep Time: 10 minutes Cook Time: 15 minutes Servings: 2-3

Ingredients:

- 1 lb (450g) button mushrooms, cleaned and stems trimmed
- 3 tablespoons olive oil
- 4 cloves garlic, minced
- 1/4 cup dry white wine
- 1 tablespoon fresh lemon juice
- 2 tablespoons chopped fresh parsley
- Salt and pepper to taste
- Crusty bread for serving

Directions:

1. Warm the olive oil in an expansive skillet over medium warm.
2. Add the minced garlic to the skillet and sauté for 1-2 minutes until fragrant.

3. Include the mushrooms in the skillet and cook for almost 5 minutes, blending sometimes, until they mollify.
4. Pour the white wine and lemon juice, and cook for another 5 minutes or until the mushrooms are delicate and the fluid has decreased.
5. Season the mushrooms with salt and pepper to taste.
6. Stir in the chopped fresh parsley and cook for an additional minute.
7. Remove the skillet from heat and transfer the Spanish Garlic Mushrooms to a serving dish.
8. Serve the mushrooms with crusty bread on the side, allowing guests to soak up the flavorful sauce.

Nutrition Info (per serving):

- Calories: 230
- Total Fat: 17g
- Saturated Fat: 2.5g
- Cholesterol: 0mg
- Sodium: 10mg
- Total Carbohydrates: 9g
- Dietary Fiber: 2g
- Sugars: 3g
- Protein: 5g

ITALIAN STUFFED TOMATOES WITH RICE AND HERBS

Prep Time: 20 minutes Cook Time: 35 minutes Servings: 4

Ingredients:

- 4 large ripe tomatoes
- 1 cup cooked white rice
- 1/4 cup finely chopped onion
- 2 cloves garlic, minced
- 2 tablespoons chopped fresh basil
- 2 tablespoons chopped fresh parsley
- 1/4 cup grated Parmesan cheese
- 2 tablespoons olive oil
- Salt and pepper to taste

Directions:

1. Preheat the stove to 375°F (190°C). Oil a prepared dish with olive oil and set aside.

2. Cut the tops off the tomatoes and scoop out the seeds and pulp, leaving a hollow cavity. Reserve the pulp and discard the seeds.
3. Mix
4. Stuff each tomato with the rice mixture, pressing it gently to fill the cavity.
5. Place the stuffed tomatoes in the prepared baking dish and drizzle them with olive oil.
6. Cover the heating dish with an aluminum thwart and prepare the tomatoes within the broiler for 25-30 minutes or until the tomatoes are delicate and the rice is completely cooked.
7. Remove the foil and bake for an additional 5 minutes to allow the tops of the tomatoes to brown slightly.
8. Serve the Italian Stuffed Tomatoes with Rice and Herbs as a delightful side dish or a light and flavorful vegetarian main course.

Nutrition Info (per serving):

- Calories: 210
- Total Fat: 8g
- Saturated Fat: 2g
- Cholesterol: 5mg
- Sodium: 120mg
- Total Carbohydrates: 28g
- Dietary Fiber: 3g
- Sugars: 4g
- Protein: 7g

MOROCCAN SPICED CAULIFLOWER

Prep Time: 10 minutes Cook Time: 25-30 minutes Servings: 4

Ingredients:

- 1 large head of cauliflower, cut into florets
- 2 tablespoons olive oil
- 1 teaspoon ground cumin
- 1 teaspoon ground coriander
- 1/2 teaspoon ground turmeric
- 1/2 teaspoon ground cinnamon
- 1/4 teaspoon ground ginger
- 1/4 teaspoon cayenne pepper (optional for added heat)
- Salt and pepper to taste
- Fresh cilantro leaves for garnish

Directions:

1. Preheat the oven to 425°F (220°C). Line a baking sheet with parchment paper or lightly grease it with olive oil.
2. In a large mixing bowl, combine the cauliflower florets with olive oil, ground cumin, ground coriander, ground turmeric, ground cinnamon, ground ginger, cayenne pepper (if using), salt, and pepper. Hurl the cauliflower until it is equally coated with the flavors and oil.
3. Spread the seasoned cauliflower in a single layer on the prepared baking sheet.
4. Broil the cauliflower on the preheated stove for 25-30 minutes or until it is delicate and softly browned, mixing once or twice amid cooking to guarantee, indeed browning.
5. Remove the roasted cauliflower from the oven and transfer it to a serving dish.
6. Garnish the Moroccan Spiced Cauliflower with fresh cilantro leaves before serving.

Nutrition Info (per serving):

- Calories: 120
- Total Fat: 7g
- Saturated Fat: 1g
- Cholesterol: 0mg
- Sodium: 80mg
- Total Carbohydrates: 13g
- Dietary Fiber: 5g
- Sugars: 5g
- Protein: 4g

GREEK SPANAKORIZO (SPINACH AND RICE)

Prep Time: 10 minutes Cook Time: 25 minutes Servings: 4

Ingredients:

- 1 cup long-grain white rice
- 2 tablespoons olive oil
- 1 medium onion, finely chopped
- 3 cloves garlic, minced
- 1 pound fresh spinach, washed and chopped
- 1 cup vegetable or chicken broth
- 1/2 cup water
- 1 tablespoon fresh dill, chopped
- 1 tablespoon fresh parsley, chopped
- 1/2 teaspoon dried oregano
- Salt and pepper to taste
- Lemon wedges for serving

Directions:

1. Rinse the rice under cold water until the water runs clear. Drain and set aside.
2. Warm the olive oil over medium warm in an expansive pot or profound skillet. Add the chopped onion and sauté until translucent, about 3-4 minutes.
3. Stir in the minced garlic and sauté for 1-2 minutes until fragrant.
4. Add the chopped spinach to the pot and cook until wilted, stirring occasionally.
5. Pour in the vegetable or chicken broth and water. Bring the liquid to a boil.
6. Stir in the rice, dill, parsley, and dried oregano—season with salt and pepper to taste.
7. Reduce the heat to low, cover the pot, and let the mixture simmer for 15-20 minutes or until the rice is tender and has absorbed the liquid.
8. Once the rice is cooked, remove the pot from the heat and let it sit, covered, for a few minutes to allow the flavors to meld.
9. Fluff the Greek Spanakorizo with a fork and serve it warm. Garnish with additional fresh dill and a squeeze of lemon juice, if desired.

Nutrition Info (per serving):

- Calories: 250
- Total Fat: 7g
- Saturated Fat: 1g
- Cholesterol: 0mg
- Sodium: 350mg
- Total Carbohydrates: 41g
- Dietary Fiber: 4g
- Sugars: 2g
- Protein: 6g

CHAPTER 6: DESSERTS

ITALIAN TIRAMISU

Prep Time: 30 minutes Chilling Time: 4 hours or overnight Servings: 6-8

Ingredients:

- 1 cup strong brewed coffee, cooled
- 3 tablespoons coffee liqueur (optional)
- 3 large egg yolks
- 1/2 cup granulated sugar
- 1 cup mascarpone cheese
- 1 cup heavy cream
- 1 teaspoon vanilla extract
- 24 ladyfinger cookies
- Unsweetened cocoa powder for dusting
- Chocolate shavings or grated chocolate for garnish (optional)

Directions:

1. In a shallow dish, mix the brewed coffee and coffee liqueur (if using). Set aside.
2. Whisk together the egg yolks and sugar in a medium-sized mixing bowl until thick and pale.
3. Include the mascarpone cheese in the egg yolk blend and tenderly crease until well combined and smooth.
4. Wash the heavy cream and vanilla extract in a separate bowl until stiff peaks form.
5. Gently fold the whipped cream into the mascarpone mixture until fully incorporated.
6. Dip each ladyfinger into the coffee mixture for a few seconds, ensuring not to soak them completely.
7. Organize a layer of splashed ladyfingers within the foot of a serving dish or personal glasses.
8. Spread half of the mascarpone mixture over the ladyfingers.
9. Repeat with another layer of soaked ladyfingers and the remaining mascarpone mixture.
10. Cover and refrigerate the Tiramisu for at least 4 hours, or overnight, to allow the flavors to meld and the dessert to set.
11. Before serving, dust the top with unsweetened cocoa powder and garnish with chocolate shavings or grated chocolate if desired.

Nutrition Info (per serving, based on 8 servings):

- Calories: 370
- Total Fat: 25g
- Saturated Fat: 14g
- Cholesterol: 185mg
- Sodium: 50mg
- Total Carbohydrates: 30g
- Dietary Fiber: 1g
- Sugars: 16g
- Protein: 6g

GREEK BAKLAVA

Prep Time: 30 minutes Cook Time: 45-50 minutes Servings: 24 pieces

Ingredients:

- 1 package (16 ounces) phyllo dough, thawed
- 1 cup unsalted butter, melted
- 2 cups mixed nuts (walnuts, pistachios, and almonds), finely chopped
- 1 teaspoon ground cinnamon
- 1/2 teaspoon ground cloves
- 1 cup granulated sugar
- 1 cup water
- 1/2 cup honey
- 1 teaspoon vanilla extract
- 1 cinnamon stick (optional)
- Zest of 1 lemon (optional)

Directions:

1. Before cooking, please turn on your oven and set it to 350°F (175°C). Spread melted butter on a baking dish that measures 9 by 13 inches.
2. Mix the chopped nuts with ground cinnamon and cloves in a bowl. Set aside.
3. Put a wet kitchen towel over the phyllo dough so it doesn't dry out.
4. Place one sheet of phyllo dough into the prepared baking dish. Brush it lightly with melted butter. Repeat this process, stacking and buttering each sheet until you have about 10 sheets layered.
5. Sprinkle a generous layer of the nut mixture (about 1/3 cup) evenly over the phyllo sheets.
6. Continue layering and buttering phyllo sheets, followed by the nut mixture, until all the nuts are used. Finish with a final layer of 10-12 phyllo sheets, each brushed with melted butter.
7. Using a sharp knife, cut the baklava into diamond or square shapes.
8. Bake in the oven for about 45-50 minutes or until the baklava turns golden brown and crisp.
9. As the baklava bakes, get the syrup ready. Mix the white sugar, water, honey, vanilla extract, cinnamon stick (if you have it), and lemon zest (if you have it). Heat the mixture until it starts to boil. Then, lower the temperature and let it cook gently for around 10 minutes.
10. Remove the cinnamon stick and lemon zest from the syrup.
11. When the baklava is done baking, immediately pour the hot syrup over the hot baklava, making sure to cover all the pieces.
12. Allow the baklava to cool completely, and soak up the syrup before serving.

Nutrition Info (per serving):

- Calories: 260
- Total Fat: 17g
- Saturated Fat: 6g
- Cholesterol: 20mg
- Sodium: 85mg
- Total Carbohydrates: 24g
- Dietary Fiber: 2g
- Sugars: 13g

- Protein: 3g

MEDITERRANEAN ORANGE AND ALMOND CAKE

Prep Time: 20 minutes Cook Time: 1 hour (for boiling oranges) + 40-45 minutes (baking) Servings: 10-12 slices

Ingredients:

- 2 large oranges
- 4 eggs
- 1 cup granulated sugar
- 2 cups almond flour
- 1 teaspoon baking powder
- 1/2 teaspoon baking soda
- Pinch of salt
- 1/2 cup olive oil
- 1/2 cup Greek yogurt
- 1 teaspoon vanilla extract
- Powdered sugar for dusting

Directions:

1. Please turn on your oven and set it to 350°F (175°C). Put a layer of grease in a cake pan that is 9 inches in diameter. Then, place parchment paper on the bottom of the pan.
2. Wash the oranges thoroughly and place them in a pot of boiling water. Boil the oranges for about 1 hour or until they are soft and easily pierced with a fork. Remove the oranges from the water, let them cool, and cut them into quarters. Remove any seeds and the white pith.
3. Blend the whole oranges (with skin) in a food processor until you get a smooth puree. Set aside.
4. In a large mixing bowl, beat the eggs and sugar until creamy and well combined.
5. Whisk the almond flour, baking powder, baking soda, and salt in a separate bowl.
6. Slowly mix the dry ingredients into the egg mixture, taking turns adding the olive oil and Greek yogurt. Mix until the batter is smooth.
7. Mix in the orange puree and vanilla extract until everything is well incorporated.
8. Put the batter into the ready cake pan and use a spatula to smooth the top.
9. Bake the cake in the oven for 40-45 minutes or until a toothpick inserted into the center comes clean.
10. Allow the cake to cool in the pan for 10 minutes. Then, move it to a wire rack to cool down completely.
11. After the cake cools down, sprinkle powdered sugar on top to make it look fancy.

Nutrition Info (per serving):

- Calories: 280
- Total Fat: 18g
- Saturated Fat: 2g
- Cholesterol: 62mg
- Sodium: 115mg
- Total Carbohydrates: 25g
- Dietary Fiber: 4g
- Sugars: 19g
- Protein: 6g

ITALIAN CANNOLI WITH RICOTTA AND CHOCOLATE

Prep Time: 1 hour Resting Time: 30 minutes Cook Time: 15 minutes Servings: 12-14 cannoli

Ingredients: For the Cannoli Shells:

- 1 cup all-purpose flour
- 2 tablespoons granulated sugar
- 1/4 teaspoon salt
- 1 tablespoon unsweetened cocoa powder
- 2 tablespoons unsalted butter, cold and cut into small pieces
- 1/4 cup sweet Marsala wine
- 1 large egg white
- Vegetable oil for frying
- Confectioners' sugar for dusting

For the Filling:

- 1 cup ricotta cheese
- 1/2 cup powdered sugar
- 1/2 teaspoon vanilla extract
- 1/4 cup mini chocolate chips
- Candied orange peel, for garnish (optional)

Directions: For the Cannoli Shells:

1. Whisk together the flour, granulated sugar, salt, and cocoa powder in a large bowl. Add the cold butter pieces and use your fingers to work the butter into the flour mixture until it resembles coarse crumbs.
2. Whisk together the Marsala wine and egg white in a separate small bowl. Gradually pour the liquid into the flour mixture and mix until a dough forms. Take the dough and shape it into a ball. Cover it with a sheet of plastic wrap and put it in the refrigerator for at least 30 minutes.
3. Roll out the dough on a lightly floured surface into a thin sheet, about 1/16-inch thick. Use a small round cutter to cut circles from the dough around 3 to 4 inches in size.
4. Wrap each dough circle around a cannoli mold or a metal tube, slightly overlapping the edges. Dab the edges with water and press to seal the seam.
5. Heat vegetable oil to 350°F (175°C) in a deep saucepan. Carefully fry the cannoli shells, a few at a time, until they are golden brown and crispy, about 1-2 minutes. Use tongs to remove the oil's covers and put them on a plate with paper towels to soak up extra fat.
6. Let the cannoli shells cool completely before removing them from the molds.

<u>For the Filling:</u>

1. Blend the ricotta cheese, powdered sugar, and vanilla extract until it becomes smooth and creamy.
2. Gently fold in the mini chocolate chips, reserving some for garnish.

<u>Assembling the Cannoli:</u>

1. Fill each cooled cannoli shell with the ricotta filling using a piping bag or a small spoon. Start from one end and pipe the filling into the surface, then repeat from the other end.

2. Garnish the ends of each cannoli with additional mini chocolate chips and candied orange peel, if desired.
3. Dust the filled cannoli with confectioners' sugar just before serving.

Nutrition Info (per serving - 1 cannoli):

- Calories: 170
- Total Fat: 8g
- Saturated Fat: 5g
- Cholesterol: 23mg
- Sodium: 39mg
- Total Carbohydrates: 21g
- Dietary Fiber: 1g
- Sugars: 9g
- Protein: 4g

GREEK YOGURT WITH HONEY AND FRESH FRUIT

Prep Time: 5 minutes. Servings: 1-2

Ingredients:

- 1 cup Greek yogurt
- 2 tablespoons honey
- Assorted fresh fruits (such as berries, sliced peaches, kiwi, or pomegranate seeds)

Directions:

1. In a bowl, spoon the Greek yogurt.
2. Drizzle the honey over the yogurt.
3. Wash and prepare the fresh fruits of your choice. Cut larger fruits into bite-sized pieces.
4. Arrange the fresh fruits on top of the yogurt.

5. Serve immediately and enjoy the refreshing and nutritious Greek Yogurt with Honey and Fresh Fruit.

Nutrition Info (per serving):

- Calories: 220
- Total Fat: 0.5g
- Saturated Fat: 0g
- Cholesterol: 5mg
- Sodium: 50mg
- Total Carbohydrates: 40g
- Dietary Fiber: 2g
- Sugars: 36g
- Protein: 17g

MOROCCAN ORANGE BLOSSOM WATER PUDDING

Prep Time: 10 minutes Cook Time: 5 minutes Chill Time: 2 hours Servings: 4

Ingredients:

- 2 cups whole milk
- 1/2 cup sugar
- 1/4 cup cornstarch
- 1/4 cup water
- 2 tablespoons orange blossom water
- 1 teaspoon vanilla extract
- Sliced almonds or pistachios for garnish (optional)

Directions:

1. Mix the sugar and cornstarch in a pot until they are well mixed.

2. Gradually add the milk to the saucepan, stirring constantly to avoid lumps.
3. Mix the water and orange blossom water in a separate small bowl, then add this mixture to the saucepan and the vanilla extract.
4. Heat the mixture on medium heat and stir it all the time. Keep cooking until it becomes thicker and begins to boil. Turn down the heat and mix the ingredients for 1-2 minutes.
5. Take the saucepan off the heat and put the pudding into either a small bowl for each person or a big bowl.
6. Allow the pudding to cool at room temperature for a few minutes, then cover with plastic wrap and refrigerate until completely chilled and set.
7. Garnish the chilled pudding with sliced almonds or pistachios before serving.

Nutrition Info (per serving):

- Calories: 180
- Total Fat: 4g
- Saturated Fat: 2g
- Cholesterol: 12mg
- Sodium: 60mg
- Total Carbohydrates: 33g
- Dietary Fiber: 0g
- Sugars: 25g
- Protein: 4g

ITALIAN LEMON RICOTTA COOKIES

Prep Time: 20 minutes Chill Time: 1 hour Bake Time: 12-14 minutes Servings: 36 cookies

Ingredients:

- 1 cup unsalted butter, softened
- 1 1/2 cups granulated sugar
- 2 large eggs
- 15 oz ricotta cheese
- 1 teaspoon vanilla extract
- Zest of 1 lemon
- 4 cups all-purpose flour
- 1/2 teaspoon baking soda
- 1/2 teaspoon salt

For the Glaze:

- 1 1/2 cups powdered sugar
- 2 tablespoons fresh lemon juice
- Zest of 1 lemon

Directions:

1. Mix the soft butter and granulated sugar in a big bowl until it becomes light and fluffy.
2. Beat the eggs individually, then add the ricotta cheese, vanilla extract, and lemon zest. Mix until well combined.
3. Mix the regular flour, baking soda, and salt in another bowl.
4. Slowly combine the dry and wet ingredients, stirring until a soft dough is made.
5. Put plastic wrap over the dough in the fridge for at least 1 hour to make it firmer.
6. Warm your oven to 350°F (175°C) and place parchment paper on a baking sheet.
7. Take a spoon or cookie scoop. Put spoonfuls of dough onto the baking sheet. Please make sure they are about 2 inches away from each other.
8. Cook the cookies in the oven for 12-14 minutes or until the edges turn golden.
9. While the cookies are cooking in the oven, get the glaze ready. Mix the powdered sugar, lemon juice, and lemon peel in a little bowl until smooth.
10. After taking the cookies out of the oven, cool them on the baking sheet before putting them on a wire rack to cool completely.
11. Drizzle the glaze over the cooled cookies using a spoon or a pastry bag.

Nutrition Info (per serving, one cookie):

- Calories: 130
- Total Fat: 6g
- Saturated Fat: 4g
- Cholesterol: 25mg
- Sodium: 55mg
- Total Carbohydrates: 17g
- Dietary Fiber: 0g
- Sugars: 9g
- Protein: 2g

GREEK LOUKOUMADES (HONEY PUFFS)

Prep Time: 1 hour 15 minutes (including resting time) Cook Time: 15 minutes Servings: Approximately 30 loukoumades

Ingredients:

- 1 1/2 cups all-purpose flour
- 1 teaspoon active dry yeast
- 1/4 teaspoon salt
- 1 cup lukewarm water
- Vegetable oil for frying

For the Syrup:

- 1 cup honey
- 1/2 cup water
- 1 cinnamon stick
- Zest of 1 lemon

For Serving:

- Chopped walnuts
- Ground cinnamon

Directions:

1. Whisk together the flour, yeast, and salt in a mixing bowl. Slowly pour the slightly warm water into the mixture and mix it well until the batter becomes smooth. Put a clean kitchen towel over the bowl and wait about 1 hour or until the batter becomes twice as big in a warm area.
2. In the meantime, prepare the syrup. Put the honey, water, cinnamon stick, and lemon peel in a saucepan together. Heat the liquid slowly until it starts to bubble gently. Then, lower the heat and let it cook quietly for 5 minutes. Take it off the stove and let it cool down.
3. After the batter has gotten bigger, heat vegetable oil in a deep frying pan to a temperature of 350°F (180°C).
4. Put small amounts of the batter into the hot oil using a spoon. Fry the loukoumades in batches, turning them occasionally with a slotted spoon, until they are golden brown and puffed up. This should take about 2-3 minutes per batch.
5. Put the loukoumades out of the oil on a plate with paper towels to eliminate extra grease.
6. While the loukoumades are still warm, dip them into the prepared syrup and coat them evenly.
7. Serve the loukoumades immediately, sprinkled with chopped walnuts and a dusting of ground cinnamon.

Nutrition Info (per serving, 3 loukoumades):

- Calories: 220
- Total Fat: 1g
- Saturated Fat: 0g
- Cholesterol: 0mg
- Sodium: 75mg
- Total Carbohydrates: 50g
- Dietary Fiber: 1g
- Sugars: 26g

- Protein: 3g

MEDITERRANEAN FRUIT SALAD WITH MINT

Prep Time: 15 minutes. Servings: 4

Ingredients:

- 1 cup watermelon, diced
- 1 cup cantaloupe, diced
- 1 cup honeydew melon, diced
- 1 cup strawberries, halved
- 1 cup blueberries
- 1 cup grapes, halved
- 1 tablespoon fresh mint leaves, chopped

For the Dressing:

- 2 tablespoons honey
- 1 tablespoon fresh lemon juice
- Zest of 1 lemon

Directions:

1. Combine the diced watermelon, cantaloupe, honeydew melon, strawberries, blueberries, and grapes in a large bowl.
2. Whisk together the honey, fresh lemon juice, and zest in a separate small bowl to make the dressing.
3. Put the dressing over the fruit and mix it gently until all the fruits are covered evenly.
4. Sprinkle the chopped fresh mint leaves over the fruit salad and toss again to incorporate the mint.
5. Put plastic wrap over the bowl in the fridge for at least 30 minutes so the flavors can mix.
6. Before serving, give the fruit salad a final toss and adjust the sweetness by adding more honey or lemon juice if desired.

Nutrition Info (per serving):

- Calories: 120
- Total Fat: 0.5g
- Saturated Fat: 0g
- Cholesterol: 0mg
- Sodium: 10mg
- Total Carbohydrates: 30g
- Dietary Fiber: 3g
- Sugars: 24g
- Protein: 1g

ITALIAN GELATO WITH FRESH BERRIES

Prep Time: 15 minutes Chilling Time: 4 hours or overnight Churning Time: 20-25 minutes Freezing Time: 2 hours Servings: 4

Ingredients:

- 2 cups whole milk
- 1 cup heavy cream
- 3/4 cup granulated sugar
- 4 large egg yolks
- 1 teaspoon pure vanilla extract
- 1 cup mixed fresh berries (strawberries, raspberries, blueberries, blackberries)
- Fresh mint leaves for garnish

Directions:

1. Mix the milk and cream in a pan on the stove with medium heat. Heat the mixture until it simmers, but do not let it boil. Remove from heat and set aside.
2. Mix the white sugar and egg yolks in a different bowl until it looks light and creamy.

3. Slowly pour the hot milk and cream mixture into the egg yolk mixture, whisking continuously to combine.
4. Put the mixture into the saucepan and heat it on medium. Keep stirring the mixture with a wooden spoon until it gets thicker and sticks to the back of the spoon. This will take around 5 to 7 minutes. Make sure it doesn't get too hot.
5. Take the pot off the stove and mix in the vanilla extract. Let the mixture cool to room temperature.
6. After it cools down, put a cover on the saucepan and place it in the refrigerator for at least 4 hours or overnight to ensure it gets cold.
7. When you are ready to make gelato, pour the cold mixture into an ice cream maker and churn it as directed by the instructions provided by the manufacturer.
8. While the gelato is churning, wash and prepare the fresh berries. Cut the strawberries into slices and leave the other berries whole.
9. After the gelato is finished mixing and becomes the texture you want, please put it in a container with a lid and gently mix in the fresh berries.
10. Cover the container with a lid and freeze the gelato for 2 hours to firm up.
11. Serve the Italian Gelato with Fresh Berries in individual bowls or cones. Add fresh mint leaves on top for a burst of color and freshness.

Nutrition Info (per serving):

- Calories: 350
- Total Fat: 20g
- Saturated Fat: 11g
- Cholesterol: 220mg
- Sodium: 50mg
- Total Carbohydrates: 35g
- Dietary Fiber: 2g
- Sugars: 30g
- Protein: 7g

Printed in Great Britain
by Amazon

35720925R00082